MW01504726

Teaching in the New Crazy

On Thriving in an Overwhelming, Politicized,
and Complicated World

GLEN COLEMAN

DEDICATION

To the teacher who inspires young people in our age of disruption: You inspire me.

Contents

Introduction

Fellow educators, we need to call it like it is. Teaching young people today is a white-knuckle drive that can make us feel as though we're losing our sanity. We're supposed to help students think critically as our democracy crumbles, as trust gives way to tribalism, and as confidence in institutions such as our elections, the dollar, or vaccines gives way to doubt. Today's debates are met with fear because the issues we face are overwhelming, politicized, and complicated. This has resulted in a new cynicism that is appearing in our classrooms.

"Why do I need to know 'this' when AI can do it for me?"

"Why learn about the world when it's falling apart?"

"Why listen to adults when they caused this mess?"

These will be constant refrains in our classrooms, if they are not already.

My response is because one lesson can still change a life. A teacher can still empower our youth to right the wrongs of previous generations. A good question can still open anyone's mind.

And yet our problems are too great for any one teacher to solve.

This realization can lead to burnout.

So, I'm writing this book to help you, regardless of what you teach — no matter where or when — and to start a conversation within our profession about how to thrive in what I will call "the new crazy," or our "chaotic new normal."

June 8, 2023
Orange Is the New Blue?

I'm writing in the book room at River Dell High School at 11:30 a.m. on June 8, 2023. It's just across the hallway from my classroom. This room — small, dark, and dingy with a tinge of mildew — is where I do most of my schoolwork when I'm not teaching.

This morning, something otherworldly happened right across the hallway, in classroom 902. The sky turned dark orange. Smoke from forest fires in Quebec has drifted south and contaminated our sky.

Now, students and teachers look at each other, bewildered.

When class had begun, students immediately took out their laptops and got to work. Midway through, on a lark I opened the shades. The sky was dark orange, like from Munch's *The Scream,* like we had landed on Mars. Students erupted, "Whoa! What the $#@! is that?!" It was one of those rare moments that create a "before and after" time stamp in your brain. Before I raised the window shades, the world had seemed normal. After I raised the window shades, the world had changed.

Students rushed to the window and took out their phones to snap pictures of the eerie sky. The entire class — really the entire school — was transfixed in this slow-motion ecological horror scene. There was a feeling of foreboding: Something was beyond our control and shocked our status quo. Our assumption of safety was violated.

Students joked on June 8, 2023:

"So this is how it ends."

"Global warming, thank you!"

"Dr. Coleman, why is this happening?"

In the back of my mind, I wondered, "How could anything so nightmarish impact upscale Oradell, New Jersey?" In 2016, Oradell was voted the best town for families in New Jersey.

My mind continued to wander. What if the sky stays dark orange for a month? What will happen to the harvest? What if the air stays thick from smoke for days? What will happen to our health?

Suddenly the Industrial Revolution — the unit we were studying — became dizzyingly relevant. Fossil fuels' impacts were right outside our window and right inside our lungs, leaving a bitter taste.

No app could save us from the smoke. No consumer product could stop the forest fires. No AI, VR, same-day delivery, or streaming service could turn the orange sky back to blue. And no one could point to La Grande Reservoir, Quebec, where the forest fires started, nor could we fathom its enormity.

All we knew was that the sky had changed. It resulted in the cancellation of after-school sports — basically the school's religion. School closed at 2:35 p.m. We wondered and agonized on June 8 ... and yet days later, we had forgotten it. We'd filed it away in our "inner mental cabinet" of chaotic events — cold cases filed away when we can't make sense of them.

As a social studies teacher, I'm supposed to make sense of the world. I'm supposed to create a classroom experience where vigorous debate and learning experiences can open the minds of young people.

When we address societal issues, students can inform themselves and think critically. Yes? Those learning experiences can help sustain our democracy, right?

The truth is (maybe I am dumb for saying this): I believe I can make a difference. I believe I can open students' minds and strengthen their voices.

I'm a romantic, a do-gooder, and a sucker. But that's teaching. You're supposed to fix it. Your course content — whether it's math or poetry — has the capacity to open students' minds. We can help our students understand their world and sharpen their critical thinking, right?

Hold onto that thought and consider the following, written by Horace Mann in 1848, an early pioneer of public education. This was his view on why we have it:

> *"Under the Providence of God, our means of education are the grand machinery by which the 'raw material' of human nature can be worked up into inventors and discoverers, into skilled artisans and scientific farmers, into scholars and jurists, into the founders of benevolent institutions, and the great expounders of ethical and theological science. By means of early education, these embryos of talent may be quickened, which will solve the difficult problems of political and economical law; and by them, too, the genius may be*

kindled which will blaze forth in the Poets of Humanity."[1]

Try not to laugh. Reread it. Please.

Was Horace smoking pot?

Did you smirk at the "embryos of talent," the "scientific farmers," the "great expounders of ethical and theological science," that lead to (drumroll, please) "Poets of Humanity"?

"Horace!" says the overwhelmed teacher writing in the book room just opposite room 902. The punchline is that the founder of our public education was high on romanticism. And so am I. And I am burning out from it.

Cultivate "Poets of Humanity?" Really? In our age of polarization?

Go to a local board of education meeting and hear the "good news" — teachers brainwash children and then take long summers off.

Maybe I'm alone. Maybe the orange sky has befuddled me. Maybe I'm at peak phone addiction. Maybe global warming, nuclear war, bioengineering, and polarization have gotten me down. But the truth is Horace was right. Public schools *are* to serve humanity. They *are* to cultivate young peoples' geniuses. It is we who've grown numb.

Yet I suspect there are still suckers for learning... .

Take, for example, the vision statement of social studies from the State of New Jersey:

---

[1] "Horace Mann: Report No. 12 of the Massachusetts School Board (1848)." *https://faculty.etsu.edu/history/documents/hmann.htm.*

Vision: An education in social studies
fosters a population that:

- <u>Is civic-minded, globally aware,</u>[my underline] and socially responsible;
- Exemplifies fundamental values of democracy and human rights through active participation in local, state, national, and global communities;
- Makes informed decisions about local, state, national, and global events based on inquiry and analysis;
- Considers multiple perspectives, values diversity, and promotes cultural understanding;
- Recognizes the relationships between people, places, and resources as well as the implications of an interconnected global economy;
- Applies an understanding of critical media literacy skills when utilizing technology to learn, communicate, and collaborate with diverse people around the world; and
- Discerns fact from falsehood and critically analyzes information for validity and relevance.[2]

The above statement is as inspiring as Horace's is naive. Both leave us in a bind: How can we encourage learners to adopt "values of democracy" when a third of the country thinks the 2020 presidential election was rigged? When respected books are banned in over thirty-

---

[2] "Social Studies." *www.nj.gov*, 2020, www.nj.gov/education/standards/socst/.

three states? When teachers are fired for asking tough questions? When mentioning global warming is seen as politicizing instruction? Or when certain words — such as *gay* — are forbidden in the classroom?

In short, how can anyone be a "Poet of Humanity" while walking on eggshells?

New Jersey's mission statement is not flawed. Neither is Horace Mann's. What's wrong is that teachers are supposed to uphold long-lost values while our society undermines them. Failing to acknowledge that problem only fuels the new crazy.

To help answer the question, "How to teach in the new crazy, or, our chaotic new normal," I have divided this book into three parts:

Part 1 - Describing our chaotic new normal. The problems we face are new and real and are borne of our mindset, our classrooms, and our world. (Interviewees in Part 3 do not all agree with my assessment, See Part 3.)

Part 2 - Strategies to navigate through the storm. I share some counterintuitive strategies that helped me get through the new crazy. Many take the form of thought experiments to get you to rethink basic assumptions. I suspect that's what our chaotic new normal will require.

Part 3 - Six Interviews. This portion of the book reflects my humility and is a tangible indication that each teacher has a valuable perspective that can help us move forward. (Again, not all teachers agreed with my assessment and those differences need to be aired.) Like many of us, I struggle in the new crazy. But to thrive now, we must ask the question, "How do we teach in our chaotic new normal?" — and nurture the community that results. So I interviewed six teachers based on that question. These interviews also prove that not everyone feels comfortable expressing themselves for fear of societal backlash. For example, of the six interviewees, one insisted on remaining anonymous due to fears that airing their views would lead to harsh consequences.

PART I

What Is Our Chaotic New Normal and How Did We Get Here?

My own path into this chaotic new normal starts with this fact: I failed the first grade. My handwriting was so bad — still is — that in my thirties I had students teach me how to print more clearly in the middle of a lesson I thought I was teaching. It's probably due to congenital visual disabilities. I saw doctors about it when I was very young. I still read slowly and ponderously. But because I take notes on what I read — and then take notes on my notes — I remember what I read.

My curse of bad handwriting lifted in the summer of 1982, just before I entered my freshman year of high school. That's when my dad brought home a personal computer, an Apple IIc. Instantly, I could read what I wrote and move my thoughts on screen.

Before the computer turned on, I thought I was a failure. After it powered up, I believed I could be successful because I could read what I wrote. With my newly liberated voice, I knew I could regain control of my life.

It also bears mentioning that my mom was a founder and principal of a religious school for Reform Judaism. She was a thinker and doer — a natural leader. Her questions flowed with beauty. They inspired me throughout my childhood. Were I to disagree with my mother, I would bring an article to the dinner table where we discussed it. So while my school said I was dumb, my mom asked me what I thought.

I learned to adore questions. They gave me the opportunity to speak my truth and claim my power. Those experiences led me to this realization:

"?" is the greatest symbol.
"?" is the symbol of growth and possibility.

At the Passover seders of my youth, idealism saturated my brain as my mom, her two sisters, and their families engaged in deep conversations. They revealed their dreams to make the world better and their nostalgia for an Israel that felt more like a movie (but tragically, did not include an empowering plotline for Palestinians). We discussed current events and their relationship to big themes like freedom, slavery, plagues, and leadership. We wondered about U.S. hostages in Iran. We meditated on biblical verses. Example: Moses killed a slave driver. How ethical was that? We sang songs with lyrics that were thousands of years old and prayed to have the strength of my great-grandparents — and that one day, Mom would sing on key.

The Passover of my youth was like *Star Wars*, which I saw when I was 10. I remember jumping up and down upon leaving the movie theater, screaming, "Use the Force!" Maybe because those Passover meals with family also strengthened a strong force within me because I was heard and could ask my elders questions.

Twenty years later, I returned to high school to teach social studies. I believed I could teach anywhere and anything because I had endured too much rejection and absorbed too much idealism to believe differently. I had bicycled across the United States twice, adventures that led me through the Great American Desert — the Midwest so named in the 1830s — over the glorious Rocky Mountains, and to the boundless Pacific. In my twenties, Woody Guthrie's *This Land Is Your Land* was my anthem. And I was ready.

So I began teaching in a public school via a new interdisciplinary course at River Dell High School, American Studies. It combined American literature with American history. With no textbook, my co-teacher and I created the course as we taught it, which was its own adventure.

(Lucky me, my co-teacher was extremely well read. She flowed with my ADD. Otherwise, that course would have flopped. Thank you, Kathy Franzino.)

But that was in 1997.
America has changed.
Teaching has changed.
I have changed.

Perhaps COVID is to blame.

Now I torment myself over witticisms said in class. Was my attempt at humor misinterpreted? Was I just videotaped?

I wonder aloud, "Aren't grades the problem, a bad target that thwarts learning?" State standards confuse me and are contradictory. Sometimes I wonder, "Am I a mental healthcare worker, a social studies teacher, or a babysitter?"

I sometimes wonder why traditional course content matters. Why know about the Civil War when we seem to be heading toward a new one? Why learn about *Hamlet* when humanity seems hell-bent on self-destruction? Why know about chemistry when we can't manage the chemicals that contaminate us?

In my own classroom at times I don't feel seen or heard.

I have watched energy in a classroom disappear with the ringing of a school bell, as if I had just been "swiped" from their phone.

I agonize, is my lesson — at best — just a droplet of hope in an ocean of indifference?

I am stunned to stammering at warp-speed technological change, yet here I am charged with preparing students for their future.

I see students getting nihilistic.

I have seen parents try to negate what I saw — their child cheated, which leaves me asking, "Is gaslighting part of our new normal?"

I find myself reading bad news only to enter school to see everyone act as if nothing had happened.

Friends say, "Retire!" But that leaves me asking, "Where else would I be able to make a living by asking deep questions?"

After twenty-six years of teaching, perhaps this has been beaten out of me, yet occasionally I'll think, "How is it that teachers are paid a pittance? Wouldn't increasing teacher pay attract greater talent, bring fresher ideas, and invigorate our mission?"

Earnest efforts to communicate are messy. So is teaching.

Today, I struggle to find a balance. Do I save myself or the children (and how can I do both?).

I bring these struggles with me — my hopes and fears — and so do you.

And yet to thrive in this chaotic new normal, we need to say what we see.

We need to ask our fellow humans: How are you? What do you see? What do you think? What should we do?

Listen intently to their answers. When met with silence, those questions can lead to burnout. But please say what you see beyond the windowpane. Unfortunately, our chaotic new normal is also defined by hard problems, meaning those our society does not seem able to fix.

(At Least) Seven Horsemen of the New Crazy

As a teacher of world civilizations for the past twenty-six years, I have, at least, a decent grasp of the sweep of world history. This has helped me understand our chaotic new normal as just that: chaotic and new, and I think it will grow more chaotic over time, throughout the next decade at least.

Here's that historical perspective to help you appreciate that today's new crazy is different from the old crazy. Historian Yuval Noah Harari, author of *Sapiens: A Brief History of Humankind* (great book), is among a number of scholars who argue that famine, plague, and

17

war defined most of history since the Agricultural Revolution, which started some 10,000 years ago. Nearly all ancient empires like those in Egypt, Mesopotamia, the Indus Valley, and China were feudal economies. Emperors or pharaohs exploited serfs. They warred to conquer land, because wealth was often viewed as a zero-sum game (*i.e.,* you or I have it).

Take the Black Death. It killed a third of Europe in three years, from 1347–1350 (the most devastating plague in history). Yet plagues were commonplace. It was the scale of the Black Death that made it unique, not the plague itself. The harsh reality was that a plague at any moment could wipe out your settlement, because it was baked into the system: The land could only produce so much. Exhaustion of the soil led to poor and unpredictable harvests, which made people vulnerable to plagues and starvation. Desperation resulted and so did wars. Famine, plague, and war were simply the yoke from which humanity could not break free.[3]

Until now...

Thank goodness modern industrial life has navigated away from the ubiquity of famine, plague, and war. Except today's problems overwhelm us instantly,

---

[3] "Thus the average person in the world of 1800 was no better off than the average person of 100,000 BC. Indeed in 1800 the bulk of the world's population was poorer than their remote ancestors. The lucky denizens of wealthy societies such as eighteenth-century England or the Netherlands managed a material lifestyle equivalent to that of the Stone Age. But the vast swath of humanity in East and South Asia, particularly in China and Japan, eked out a living under conditions probably significantly poorer than those of cavemen."

Clark, Gregory. A Farewell to Alms: A Brief Economic History of the World (The Princeton Economic History of the Western World Book 27) (p. 1). Princeton University Press. Kindle Edition.

globally, and addictively. They stream into our phones 24/7, "screaming" of armageddon because we face hard problems as algorithms, whether from social media, news sites, or YouTube, sow outrage to fuel engagement, which breaks down the reasoned conversations we need to function as a democratic society. Ironically and tragically, we know the solutions: minimize carbon emissions; regulate AI and social media; and stop the proliferation of weapons of mass destruction. And we know the havoc that will come if we don't take action: societal collapse. (Some of the interviewees in Part 3 disagree with my assessment but I will continue with my limited understanding.)

So we are left with a unique sensation today. We see global crises sweeping across the world in slow motion like on Doppler radar. Yet we also sense that no matter how informed we are, no matter how extensive our social network, and no matter how deeply we feel impending disaster, our society can't seem to fix them.

Today, there may be 1,000 "horsemen of the apocalypse." I will address only 7 to demonstrate that we are in a unique age of disruption, a new crazy. These problems are psychologically overwhelming and hard to solve.

Here they are: 1) increasing global warming, 2) continued use of plastics, 3) unchecked bioengineering, 4) unregulated AI, 5) growing threat of nuclear war, 6) rising automation in the job market, and 7) hardening and deepening polarization.

Global warming is creating an Anthropocene[4] that some fear could lead to mass extinction of life on Earth. When my students and I saw the dark orange sky on that June day, we thought, "How could forest fires happening so far away impact us here?" No one knew where Lebel-sur-Quévillon, Quebec, was. It's because, more often than not, humans fail to understand that what is out of sight may be as important as what is right in front of us. In other words, your fossil fuel-burning car (and the fossil-based economy that makes it) releases carbon that contributes to global warming, which leads to more frequent and severe forest fires, which also release tons of CO_2. (My friend and colleague whom I interview in Part 3 challenges that premise, but I'll proceed with my limited understanding here.)

Global warming is a "perfect" hard problem (because generally humans are short-term thinkers for immediate gain, while global warming is a long-term problem requiring collective action without a satisfying payoff). This combination of the science with clear solutions, and ecological disasters that stream into our phones while citizens fail to work together to solve it is characteristic of the new crazy

Plastics: Perhaps you didn't get the memo. You're eating plastic. It's in everything. It's in your fruit, vegetables, meat, and your bloodstream.[5] And it's in the

---

[4] "Anthropocene." *Education*, National Geographic, education.nationalgeographic.org/resource/anthropocene/. Accessed 1 Aug. 2023.
[5] Parker, Laura. "Microplastics Are Invading Our Bodies. How Severe Is the Damage?" *Environment*, National Geographic, 8 May 2023,

shampoo you probably use that drains into and poisons the oceans. There's no surgeon general's warning at the supermarket that reads, "This plastic is destroying our oceans and health!" It's because upfront convenience short circuits critical thinking. Plastic is so cheap to make and so easily thrown out. It's like roads and cars: impossible to avoid in today's society. But like a soda bottle that takes 500 years to decompose, the problem of plastics will grow at scale.

Isn't it strange that the substance that gives us wealth also destroys our health, and can't be substituted for anything else?

Bioengineering: If you don't know about CRISPR, you've been asleep. I'm jealous — please share. CRISPR reprograms DNA, making gods of scientists. A high school student can do the reprogramming. With the right equipment, you can reprogram a genetic code from "ABCDEFG" to a gene sequence of "ABCDMaybePlaying GodIsNotTheBestIdea?"

This technology is mind-bending. It will cure diseases, extend human life, and create new crops that are resistant to disease and drought. CRISPR may be the most powerful technology ever. But in the hands of a bad actor who creates a virulent virus or a good actor who destabilizes the ecosystem with a "well-intentioned" virus, CRISPR could indeed produce a genetically modified maelstrom, especially with the help of AI.

(Perhaps we got a sneak peak of CRISPR's chaotic effects with the outbreak of COVID-19 in 2020 when the

---

www.nationalgeographic.com/environment/article/microplastics-are-in-our-bodies-how-much-do-they-harm-us.

world shut down, as it seems to have ushered in our chaotic new normal)

AI is the first invention to generate its own "thoughts," whose intelligence grows double exponentially. AI works on projects you don't assign it to. It lies like a psychopath (meaning without telltale signs that it's lying). And it can do many heady tasks better than most humans (for example, writing a college essay), that threatens the livelihoods of many educated workers, such as lawyers and accountants.[6] Wouldn't it be disruptive if our "digital personal assistant" with a 20,000+ IQ eventually took our jobs and unbeknownst to us flooded our feeds with false news, like during an election?

Automation is when robots do work once completed by humans. Yet a funny thing is we have come to identify ourselves by our work. It's the first thing asked on a date: "What do you do?" It's also what many of us spend most of our time doing. Automation will cause most of us to redefine our relationship to work because it will change or take many of our jobs.

This brings to mind a serious question: Until what age and at what speed can one be reeducated?

A brief example: I understand that AIs can read CT scans better than most radiologists, *i.e.,* highly trained medical doctors. Yet AIs improve exponentially. They don't need love, sleep, post-secondary education, health insurance, or a hefty salary to pay off student loans. So,

---

[6] Kochhar, R. (2023, July 26). *Which U.S. workers are more exposed to AI on their jobs?*. Pew Research Center. https://www.pewresearch.org/social-trends/2023/07/26/which-u-s-workers-are-more-exposed-to-ai-on-their-jobs/

what happens to radiologists who are squeezed out of the market because of automation? What will happen to our jobs and way of life? Could that have a chaotic impact on our society, our views of education, or our American Dream? .

Nuclear war: It's a possibility we don't often talk about. For context, let's put this guy on the dollar bill: Stanislav Petrov.

On September 26, 1983, radar systems in Soviet Russia indicated that five nuclear-armed missiles were launched from the United States and heading toward the USSR. Stanislav Petrov manned that radar system.

Had he followed orders and sent a report to his commanders, they would have ordered Petrov to fire nuclear weapons at the United States. This would have started a global nuclear war.

Instead, Petrov waited 25 minutes. He thought, "It makes no sense that a nuclear war would start with only five missiles." As the minutes ticked past twenty-five, everyone in the room realized there was a glitch in the system. Petrov is the most underrated hero in human history, who by disobeying orders saved the world.

How many Petrovs are there? What if an AI mans the trigger?

Polarization: We know lies spread six times faster than truths on social media. We know those with extreme views are more likely to post to social media than those with moderate views. This has resulted in a toxic national discourse that "viralizes" conspiracy, demonizes political opponents, destroys our shared understanding of the world, and therefore smothers basic trust between people.[7] This is at the heart of the new crazy. If we can't talk about what we see and what is true without being demonized then our democracy will no longer function. Our civilization will be imperiled. Chaotic indeed.

What's worse — as if that weren't heavy enough — these seven horsemen of the apocalypse may not be fixed even if polarization is, which is the most chaotic aspect of all: a general feeling of helplessness can emerge. No March on Washington can stop a rogue actor from launching nuclear weapons. No president can stop the mass production of plastics. No regulation can contain every "CRISPR-virus." No Gretta Thurnberg can stop global warming. And no Elon Musk can stop the proliferation of AI. These seven horsemen — and there are so many others — are new and chaotic in their effect on us and our society.

Yet still, our job should be to continue to crank the engines of civic engagement. Instead, many of us understandably maintain professional silence to survive the job, choking back our words in order not to offend or overwhelm — as do many of our students — abiding so strictly to a curriculum so as to mute conversation or curiosity. As one of my interviewees attests — a teacher of social studies — they refused to reveal their real name for fear of negative professional consequences.

This then leads to the final aspect of our chaotic new normal: our classrooms.

---

[7] Center for Humane Technology. "Ledger of Harms." Humanetech.com, 2018, ledger.humanetech.com/ updated 2021.

Feeling Alone Amongst Many: Observations on the Perils of Teaching Today

The way I see it, one impediment to teaching at our best is in this expression, faulty math: Most of us are in 1 classroom alone, teaching 1 subject to 25 to 30 students, 4 or 5 times a day, 5 days a week, 180 days a year. Stuck with this systemic isolation, we may find ourselves numb with feelings of quiet desperation. Embarrassingly, I'm not sure I know what it looks like to feel supported by colleagues, administrators, parents, or the community in which I teach because solitude is normal for teachers. (In a society that suffers from an epidemic of loneliness, that's saying something.)[8]

Perhaps at some point you've had these thoughts: you said the wrong thing to your students or a colleague; you feared being recorded in class; you felt exhausted from angry parents (or angry students with no parents); you raged at sacrificing your weekends to grade papers or lesson plan; you struggled balancing your second or third job against teaching, let alone time with family; you wondered how to teach amid contradictory expectations between promoting social-emotional learning and content mastery; you've grappled with how to keep

---

[8] Office of the Assistant Secretary for Health (OASH). "New Surgeon General Advisory Raises Alarm about the Devastating Impact of the Epidemic of Loneliness and Isolation in the United States." U.S. Department of Health and Human Services, 3 May 2023, www.hhs.gov/about/news/2023/05/03/new-surgeon-general-advisory-raises-alarm-about-devastating-impact-epidemic-loneliness-isolation-united-states.html

students' attention; and you've dreaded checking email for fear of getting "that" email.

Furthermore, today's isolation is made worse from new sources of anxiety. Today, students are being set up by political activists to secretly videotape teachers in the classroom to expose their "lies, corruption, and abuse."[9] Today, we're made anxious by the prospect of addressing something controversial that pops up in class discussion.

God forbid you say the word *gay* or imply that slavery was not a picnic. Fear is contagious. It causes an epidemic of self-censorship and it may well contaminate my classroom at River Dell High School, because right next door, in Westwood, New Jersey, their board of education considered a policy that required controversial topics to first be approved by the superintendent before they could be addressed in the classroom.[10]

I spoke to a colleague who lives in Westwood and who attended their board of education meetings. She shook as she described the contentious atmosphere there.

Had the fascism I had read about in history books come to my doorstep? "I can't say the wrong thing," I thought. "Don't ask too many questions. Keep your head down, say nothing, see nothing, know nothing."

---

[9] NJ.com, Tina Kelley | NJ Advance Media for. "N.J. Activist Offers Hidden Cameras for Kids to Record 'Lies, Corruption, Abuse' in Schools." Nj, 28 June 2023, www.nj.com/education/2023/06/nj-activist-offers-hidden-cameras-for-kids-to-record-lies-corruption-abuse-in-schools.html #:~:text=0. Accessed 31 Mar. 2024.

[10] Noda, Stephanie . "Here's Where Westwood School Candidates Stand in District Fired up by Parental Rights." *North Jersey Media Group*, 1 Nov. 2023, www.northjersey.com/story/news/bergen/westwood/2023/11/01/parental-rights-has-shaken-up-westwood-nj-schools-now-voters-weigh-in/71334240007/. Accessed 31 Mar. 2024.

I pondered a superintendent approving the discussion of controversial issues. Controversial according to whom and to what end? Isn't public school supposed to help students become civic-minded and globally aware?

Shouldn't students and teachers together decide what they think is interesting, not the superintendent? Finally, how does censoring a conversation in the classroom help students get a job or become better citizens?

Just news of self-censoring crushes the will to teach. Today's chaotic new normal would make Horace Mann whimper.

We are overworked and reviled.

We are expected to promote tolerance while limiting wide-ranging conversations in our classrooms.

We are expected to grow as professionals yet are compelled to keep our anxieties secret.

We are supposed to work overtime, with scarce time in school to lesson plan, grade, or collaborate with colleagues. We see that teaching is a market failure. Money alone does not improve performance, yet epiphanies in the classroom do not percolate from a culture riddled with anxiety and poverty.

We fear that distrust is spreading between teachers, students, parents, and the larger communities we serve

We struggle to prepare students for a world that is changing too fast to be comprehended.

Finally, we realize our students have it worse than we do.

Students feel more lonely, anxious, and depressed and are more likely to self-harm than previous generations. With prolonged cell phone usage, young people are more likely to experience online bullying; lower self-esteem; objectification; shorter attention spans; less brain mass; eating disorders; and reduced feelings of trust, empathy, and closeness to other humans. Our students are more likely to feel at home on their phones than anywhere else without one. The mere presence of a cell phone is enough to lower IQs.[11][12]

The surgeon general's recent warning is alarming of loneliness as a national epidemic — more damaging than smoking a pack of cigarettes a day. These trends have compounded since 2020, when millions of students switched to online instruction at home to stop the spread of COVID-19.

My point is (with less-than-obvious solutions): Students face a lot of challenges that few teachers understand and many feel powerless to address. (A good first step: Ban students from bringing cellphones to school. Logical, right?) And herein the chaos starts to take shape: we are at a loss of what to do to help our students.

Traditional formulas fall short. The Golden Rule (*do unto others as you would have them do unto you*) could now be a recipe for career suicide. It fails to account for

---

[11] Center for Humane Technology. "Ledger of Harms." Humanetech.com, 2018, ledger.humanetech.com/. updated 2021.
[12] Ward, Adrian, et al. "Brain Drain: The Mere Presence of One's Own Smartphone Reduces Available Cognitive Capacity." Journal of the Association for Consumer Research, vol. 2, no. 2, Apr. 2017, www.hendrix.edu/uploadedFiles/Academics/Faculty_Resources/Teaching_and_Learning/Presence-Smartphone-reduces-cognitive-capacity.pdf, https://doi.org/10.1086/691462.

the fact that our students' experiences are different from our own.

We need a Golden Rule for Teachers: *Listen unto students as you would want students to listen unto you*. (This is culturally loaded. Listening is culturally nuanced. But it's a start.) In other words, give students the opportunity to teach you about them.

It's so "easy" to self-censor when the world says "shut up." But that would make us rudderless.

We need to say what we see and listen to each other to allow for new possibilities.

Additional Thoughts on The New Crazy

The new crazy is real. It's in our heads, our classrooms, and our world.

The colleagues I interviewed for Part 3 suggest ways to navigate through.

In the next section, Part 2, I describe my approach to teaching in this chaotic new normal.

In short, take good care of your mental and physical health, create a climate of trust in the classroom, and engage students to "fail forward with their friends, and with meaningful feedback, try again," a slogan I've created to summarize my approach to teaching. This is not easy. But with conversation and sharing, we can help each other.

One more thing: If I had a magic wand, (aside from increasing teacher pay), I would make all courses interdisciplinary. Combine English with history, math with science, etc. It would bring teachers from different disciplines together to reimagine their craft. It would help cure the solitude that defines our job. And it would make us less territorial and more prone to engage in collegial conversations that would renew our profession.

Final point: AI is the ultimate interdisciplinary technology. It distills all knowledge, (*i.e.,* text, images, programming, art, etc.), into 1s and 0s. In other words, it doesn't "see" the curricular walls that have defined public education for the past 100 years. If students are to become proficient with AI, they will have to start thinking interdisciplinarily, outside the box, and in new and interesting ways.

So, why not create interdisciplinary courses to better prepare students to engage in today's world?

Everyone would benefit.

PART II

How to Navigate Through Our Chaotic New Normal

Before Entering the Classroom

Just smile. A smile says, "We can do this...." I'm thinking of people who have a spine amid serious challenges. I'm thinking of Navy SEALs. They are trained to solve problems while sleepless, cold, and far from home. I bet the SEALs have a sharpened sense of humor.

I think of Joe Montana's final drive in Super Bowl XXIII. He famously engaged in small talk in the huddle just before the last, decisive play: "Hey, isn't that John Candy in the stands?" he said with a wry smile.

I think of Volodymyr Zelensky after Russia invaded Ukraine, who simply and calmly said to his people, "I am here."

I think of Nelson Mandela, who endured twenty-seven years in prison while keeping his poise.

I think of my mom, who made Passover come to life with her questions while hyperactive kids ran around the house.

The above stories inspire me. Knowing I can create a can-do mindset is step one. Cultivate that outlook. Claim your power.

There are legions of people who smile through adversity. I want their mettle.

At the end of the day, I want a rudder, a compass, and a smile through a storm.

I get it: Most students are in it only for the grade.

I get it: I'm replaceable.

I get it: Most people don't care.

I get it: Most students look at me like I'm a UFO.

I get it: Most people believe in UFOs.

I get it: We're cooked.

I get it: Professional silence is normal.

I get it: Teaching algebra or Latin makes no sense on a sinking ship.

I get it: I need to feel meaning in this life, and this book is one attempt to get it.

But smiles are a superpower. They speak of a positive attitude when things go south.

Teach students to welcome discomfort when learning something new and they'll become resilient. (Same with teachers.)

Find the funny in SNAFUs ("military speak" for Situation Normal All F*cked Up).

Develop teamwork, grit, and a sense of humor, and our day will be better.

Winning the Morning

Two years ago I was awfully depressed. I saw a psychiatrist and took meds, but they didn't work. What brought me back to wellness and an ability to press on was a daily practice of:

1. Taking a cold shower in the morning,
2. Viewing early-morning sunlight, and
3. Doing a teensy bit of early morning exercise.

The point is you can't teach well unless you're awake. I don't mean "sleepy awake." I mean Stoked! Raring to go! Booyah! Yeehaw! A.W.A.K.E.!

And the truth is, most of us don't know what that means, including me for most of my life. "Sleepy awake" was my normal. But then I listened to Andrew Huberman's podcast and learned these three techniques to achieve well-being in the morning. Huberman is a scientist at Stanford University whose goal is to bring science-based tools for everyday life to laypeople.

Cold exposure: Search "Andrew Huberman cold exposure." You'll find tons of videos of him explaining the benefits of cold showers in the morning. Cold exposure increases dopamine, the hormone that fuels motivation. That means a cold shower or ice bath can make you feel wide awake First. Thing. In. The. Morning.

Consider Tony Robbins, the world's most famous personal coach and author of *Awaken the Giant Within*. He starts each morning by plunging himself into 57° water. He says, "Boom! Every cell in the body wakes up."[13] To awaken the giant within, first awaken the body.

For the past year, daily, two-minute cold showers have invigorated my mornings. There's a jolt for 10 to 15 seconds, but with deep breaths, it's doable.

Since I realized the shock releases adrenaline and dopamine throughout my body, I've come to smile through the cold. "Cold? What cold?" This initial

---

[13] Ferriss, Tim. "Tony Robbins on Morning Routines, Peak Performance, and Mastering Money (#37 & #38)." The Blog of Author Tim Ferriss, 15 Oct. 2014, tim.blog/2014/10/15/money-master-the-game/. Accessed 31 Mar. 2024. 0:20 minutes.

discomfort results in a can-do mindset and elevation of my physical and mental well-being. (Check out Anna Lembke's book *Dopamine Nation* for added context on the science of finding balance in an age of indulgence.)

Exposure to early-morning light: Most people in industrialized societies spend too much time on screens that mess with their internal clocks that regulate sleep. As Huberman explains, what brings the body to wakefulness is natural, early-morning sunlight. It activates the pineal gland to secrete hormones like dopamine and adrenaline. This awakens each cell in the body. Huberman is clear: There is no substitute for viewing sunlight. You can't get it by looking through your bedroom window, car windshield, or indoor lighting. So get outside first thing in the morning.

Experiment: Instead of going straight from your car to your classroom, first take a fifteen-minute walk outside. Give yourself the opportunity to experience early-morning light for fifteen to twenty minutes. You'll find an increased feeling of wakefulness and calmness. With that little dose of sunlight, you may find yourself saying "Booyah!" upon entering the class.

Morning exercise: To really win the day, you may need the third essential hack, which is some kind of early-morning exercise. Nothing crazy. Here are two hacks that have made a difference for me.

Hack No. 1: I have a 50-pound kettlebell in my car. When I drive to school, I often walk down to the athletic field with my kettlebell. (There's no one there except me and a 75-year-old fella who does sprints every morning.) On my phone I set a time for one minute. I walk with the kettlebell in, let's say, my left hand. Once the timer rings, I put the kettlebell down and switch to the right hand and walk for another minute with the kettlebell. I do that for 15 minutes, walking around the track by switching the kettlebell from one hand to the other, each minute.

I'm going for slight discomfort, slight muscle fatigue in my forearms, a bit of heavy breathing. The adrenaline awakens me and helps me win the day.

Furthermore, I walk with the kettlebell in any temperature. Colder is more energizing. A walk under a clear blue sky elevates my mood.

Hack No. 2: Sometimes I bicycle to work. It feels great, like I'm an explorer traveling to a new land. I get all three protocols done in one fell swoop: 1) morning sunlight, 2) exercise, and 3) cold exposure (when biking on a cold day).

My biggest challenge was waking up early, at 6:30 a.m. I've hated mornings since birth. Waking up at 7 a.m. or later seemed predestined. Then I cracked the code upon listening to Andrew Huberman: I put a powerful light beside my bed and set it to a timer to turn on at 6 a.m. Now I am comfortably awake at 6:30. This has given me enough time to take a cold shower, pack my bike, and leave by 7 a.m. for my 6.5-mile bike ride to school.

If you have a hard time waking up in the morning (who doesn't?), consider putting a lamp by your bed. Set it to a timer to help you hack your morning.

Remember the three protocols: 1) Experiment with a cold shower. 2) View early-morning sunlight. 3) Do a teensy bit of exercise first thing in the morning. These experiences have helped put a smile on my face before I enter the classroom.

First Steps into the School: On Colleagues

When entering the school, you will meet coworkers. They are assets through any storm. A smile, a high five, a warm greeting, a fist bump, a hug — these forge community, no matter the architecture or schedule that isolates us.

We need allies, not gossip. We want to find everyone likable, even if they make you puke. Teaching is hard, in a chaotic new normal, nearly impossible. Playing nice is your vaccine.

When a colleague has experienced a death in the family or other tragedy, I call them on the phone or send a text to lend my support. Though we may not be close, these interactions say, "I like and respect you. I'm here for you."

When you work alongside someone for decades, formality gives way to familiarity. Keep that in mind when you pass a colleague in the hallway. Build bridges, not walls. Exchange good will.

Another thing: I like high fives and fist bumps. I like the connection they can create. A little swagger also goes a long way, and the truth is, swagger can be comic relief. Milk it. Energy radiates outward: "It's raining poop but I got a smile on my face."

A final point: I have had some successful collaborations with colleagues, whether in my classroom, my podcast, while interviewing for this book, schmoozing during prep, or dining at a restaurant with them. When I inquire into someone else's views, I feel more alive. I've been socially awkward since birth. But that feeling of awkwardness subsides when I show interest in someone else.

Care about others. Evoke smiles from your crew. They'll help get you through.

Make Everyone Feel Welcome, Especially Students

Keep this in mind: While you could know your colleagues for decades, you might only know your students for days. There's a transient quality to the student-teacher relationship that makes it urgent and tenuous. I have taught freshman world history for the past twenty-six years. Rarely have I taught the same students for more than two years in a row. Students frequently enter my class from other classes, school districts, states, or countries.

That transient quality of the student-teacher relationship, while normal, is compounded by the fact that ours is a transient society. Historically (going back thousands of years) it was not normal to travel across a continent for a job. But today it is. This tendency devastates the intergenerational communities that cushion life's blows, such as with grandparents, uncles, and extended family. So, appreciate the "placelessness" that your students may feel. Be a catalyst for creating or modeling strong social bonds by simply saying hello and caring to listen.

When I enter the school, I give fist bumps. My mom would tell me it's important for students to know that you like them, regardless of whether or not they like you. My mom's point was that students need to know that they are welcome in your classroom because that's the job. Your students need to know they are safe; they are invited to make mistakes and try again, because learning is a "Shawshank slog" (movie reference of crawling through manure-filled drain pipes) until morning sunlight.

There's a larger point that goes beyond the "placelessness" that many Americans feel. Because many of our towns lack infrastructure to hang out physically, such as in piazzas in Italy, students often find their community online. While at times helpful, it can also deteriorate their mental health. We know that the rates of depression among young people have skyrocketed alongside the growth of social media. This brings a triple whammy: 1) addictive engagement in an ever-hyper stimulating environment, which 2) increases pressure on students to meet impossible (anti?) social standards online, 3) that further results in their deepening feelings of isolation.

Appreciate that for most of human history — 100,000 years or so — humans lived in hunter-gatherer societies that comprised about 100 people. Now compare that to today. Students compete against billions of people to look the most attractive, fit, strong, and witty. This is made more toxic with AI filters that further distort students' self-perceptions of beauty.

In other words, students are not just competing against other people. They are now comparing themselves to impossible standards generated by ever smarter AIs that artificially make children look more "attractive" to strangers.

Again, saying hello and listening can be a lifeline.

Last year, I walked down the hallway to my classroom first thing in the morning. Every day, the same student said to me, "Good morning, Dr. Coleman!" and I responded, "Good morning, Dr. Puppy." It was an inside joke that made our day better — frequent and regular contact with another human being. "It's going to be a good day" is what we were saying to each other. To teach in chaotic times, focus on what's in front of you — focus on who's in front of you

And yet a smile does not suffice. The social contract between schools, our students, and society is strained. In Detroit in the 1950s, an assembly line worker at the Ford Motor Company could provide for a family of four and pay for the kids' college tuition.[14] Now most families require two income earners who barely hang on in an increasingly economically divided world, as the cost of living and college skyrocket. Furthermore, lacking is the assurance that good jobs await college graduates.

---

[14] Jacobson, L. (2016, January 25). *Could a GM worker afford college tuition on just two weeks' work in 1965?* Politifact.
https://www.politifact.com/factchecks/2016/jan/25/martin-omalley/could-gm-worker-afford-college-tuition-just-two-we/

And this is square one: A smile and a fist bump won't assuage the crises, but they can help create the community that cushions life's blows. No one benefits from going nuts or hollering that the apocalypse is nigh. But everyone benefits when there is a feeling of poise, reassurance, and concern from our colleagues, students, and families. That acknowledgement matters when things go sideways: We are not ignoring what is happening. We are focusing on what we can control. We're here for each other.

A fist bump or saying hello in the hallway says we'll do our best to get through this. Yes, global warming, AI, and polarization blow chunks. But we're here for each other.

Give a smile to your crew. (That's job one.) It starts with saying hello.

A Quixotic Mission Statement: You Are a Sucker

You have to understand, you're a sucker. You believe learning can change the world, a question can inspire an idiot, a joke can lighten the mood, and wonder is a drug. But you wake up, hear the news, and get depressed. Then you enter the classroom and their youth intoxicates you because they have something you don't: Energy. Wonder. You know even the most burnt-out student will wake up to a thoughtful question. Because questions cue adventure: What will happen? Why are we here? What should we do? Where are we going?

No matter whether you are a Jew, a Muslim, an atheist, or a Hindu, you have the spirit of a Jesuit within you, the highly educated soldiers for Christ who sailed around the world to spread the word of Jesus in the 1500s. My point is not Jesus. It's having the gall to sail around the world without a map for a hunch. They knew they would be greeted with open arms, violence, or worst of all, nothing — no sight of land.

But those Jesuits boarded those ships determined to explore and spread the "good word." Of course, there were moral outrages, such as their participation in the slave trade. But as a metaphor only, as a somewhat awkward symbol for teaching, we "board that ship" every time we enter the classroom with hope and flawed assumptions.

We may wonder: What if a student wants to study something forbidden? What if their interest destroys the class? What if cultivating their wonder could get you fired? But like a Jesuit of old, you set sail because the journey is you. It seduces you, the ocean. The Question (?) is your white whale: What do you think? What should we do? How do we know? But another pesters: Will you be able to navigate your class through the storms of societal dysfunction to help students learn something new?

The laughter of children, their surprise upon learning something new, their tender view of the world, their eye contact that speaks of surprise, their punchlines no matter how stilted, their get-up-and-go or hair-trigger boredom, their astonishment upon achieving mastery, cries for dispensation, and recklessness — this is the adventure.

But ...

We might not get there. We might find ourselves stranded, dehydrated, or lost. But you have something a Jesuit could only pray for: a school bell that signals the end of the day. We can try again tomorrow. Go home. Take a shower. Make dinner. Enjoy your family and friends.

But don't be shy, oh sucker. You will be disappointed. Your students, their parents, the administration, the world, and you yourself will frustrate you to no end. But learning with young people is the antidote.

Even if a meteor is hurtling to destroy planet Earth, take out a lawn chair and marvel at its majesty. Everything, absolutely everything, is fascinating. And you are lucky enough to explore that with young people.

I think of Tommy Emmanuel, the greatest acoustic guitar player ever. He's a sucker for music. He knows he can open hearts with his tone, virtuosity, and smile. He travels around the world playing at sold-out venues. He might fall short of his expectations — not that I've heard it, but he is human. Perhaps he has bad days. Perhaps an audience disappoints him. Perhaps a heatwave sucks the life out of the city or news on the street is bad. But Tommy plays because he believes. He knows, music elevates the soul. The Word — The Music — is him, and he is The Word, even in crisis, *especially* in crisis, because he knows, spirituality is work. So, he makes the journey every morning (in practice) and every night (in performance).

I think of *Field of Dreams,* a movie about a sucker for baseball. His family moves to a remote farm in Iowa. Dad, the protagonist played by Kevin Costner, has a harebrained scheme to build a baseball field in the middle of his farm. Everyone tells him he's nuts, except his wife. The baseball field cuts into the bottom line. Bankruptcy looms. A question emerges: What's more important, pursuing the dream or paying the bills? Our hero persists with the dream. While making final improvements on the baseball field, he hears a voice from the heavens, "If you build it, they will come." And they do. In the movie's final scene, people from all over Iowa come to see the beautiful game on his baseball field in endless farm country. The family is saved.

Tommy Emmanuel is a Jesuit for Music. Kevin Costner's character is a Jesuit for Baseball. We are Jesuits for Learning. We make something from nothing. Faith makes it happen, not in scripture, not in a deity or a nation, but in a process.

Questions spark interest. They open hearts and minds. If we ask it, they will come. If we listen, they will grow. It's the intangible qualities that electrify us: the wonder, the energy, the trust, the conversation, the frustration, the high fives, the laughter, the tears, the look and sound of epiphany.

Have faith that your lessons will be paid forward.

Have faith that kindness and inquiry in your classrooms will live beyond the school bell.

Make sure your compass is set to true north, oh sucker ... I mean, Jesuit for Learning. It is wonder. Make sure that your students are provisioned with a sense of humor and hearty constitution, because the journey is long and rough. Make sure you get a good night's sleep. Take a cold shower in the morning. Get ready. The bell has rung. Class has begun and you won't know where it will go.

Learning as a Holistic Act

Create energy from the get-go.

Learning requires tons of energy, and that means we have to physically move to create it. If we are physically awake, then we can be emotionally open and mentally sharp. Learning starts at the quadriceps (one of our largest muscle groups), which, when activated, energize our dopaminergic (by exercise) and "oxytonic" systems (I think I just invented a word to imply we're creating community through oxytocin) to summon the energy to learn. (See Wendy Suzuki's scholarship on the role of movement and learning.)

First and foremost, facilitate as much structured physical movement as possible in the beginning of a class to awaken and energize. This can take many forms. For example, generate laughter. It's a physical act. Laughing your ass off can get you a six-pack ... if you have *loooowww* standards.

Perhaps a better idea: games can raise heart rates, such as Simon Says, heads-shoulders-knees-toes, yoga poses, clapping rhythmically. We often do calf raises (heel on the floor to standing on tippy toes). We do 50 in a row

= a good wake-up. Get a slight lactic acid burn in the calf muscle. Nothing crazy. Just awaken the body.

Learning happens from head to toe, from head to heart. It has the power to focus our minds, move our bodies, and create community. (This is my North Star, especially in a storm.)

First-Minute Rituals at the Start of Class

A fundamental question arises when the opening bell rings: How do I invite students to work with a smile and get them interested in something that is outside their ken?

This needs to be communicated first: I care about you and what you think.

But this begs a second question: How do I get students on the same page to listen to each other?

My answer is we need a physical act or ritual that excites the body to invite the learning.

These four rituals can get the body, heart, and mind engaged in the first minute of class:

1. Sitting on desks
2. Exercise
3. Heads, Shoulders, Knees, Cup
4. Jokes

Sitting on Desks

At the very beginning of class, I often ask students to sit on their desks and face the back of the classroom. (My classroom has desks and chairs that are not connected to each other.) So they 1) stand up, 2) sit on their desks, 3) put their feet on their chairs, and 4) face the back of the classroom. This creates body language that is conducive to listening: naturally leaning forward, putting their elbows on their knees, and looking straight ahead without distraction.

Students report that they like sitting on their desks in the beginning of class because it allows them to move their bodies. They feel more comfortable and awake when they sit on their desks. It's different — divergent. They experience their classroom from a different point of view.

I like that it "awakens the room."

Rarely do I need to say more than this: "All right, sit on your desk and face the back." We do it at once. Then listening becomes a physical experience. Get out of your seat, sit on your desk, put your feet on the chairs, and look at me. Now they are focused on me.

Now I can focus their attention back onto them. Now they can listen to each other. I can ask a simple question to start: "How are you?" By listening to their answers we can go where the conversation takes us.

Exercise to Boost Energy

Perhaps the greatest obstacle facing students is fatigue. Fortunately, a *teeeeensy-weeeeeensy* bit of exercise at the beginning of class elevates students' energy, focus, and engagement.

We'll exercise an average of three days a week with the goal of creating a slight lactic acid burn, a slight increase in heart rate, and a chuckle. A feeling of community emerges.

If a student protests, "I'm tired!" I'll respond: "Precisely! In 60 seconds you'll be awake. See what happens if you stand up. Try it."

Most students buy in. More than 85% report that they like the exercise as a group ritual because it works. If someone doesn't want to, awesome. Do you. Always. No problem.

Some easy exercises to start the day:

1. Toe raises. Easy peasy. Fifty in a row is like a cup of coffee.
2. Small arm circles, both directions. Goal: get a little lactic acid in the shoulders. Do it for a minute. Reverse the direction. Smile. Then self-hugs to welcome the day.
3. Yoga chair pose for a minute: feet and knees together, hands are raised above heads with palms facing each other. Now bend the butt an inch from the chair. Raise and lower the butt 1

inch every 15 seconds. Fantastic. Good for a slight chuckle and burn in the quadriceps.

4. Simon Says = Priceless.

The goal is always fun, a smile, wakefulness, and creating a positive, welcoming spirit.

If students say they're bored by your exercises, check your sense of humor. Use exercise to help you and your students feel alive and enjoy the moment.

To be awake, move.

There are so many ways to get students on the same page in the first minute of class. Here's a good activity. Google "Head, Shoulders, Knees, Cup." Simple game. Instead of using a cup, I use a note card. I fold the card in half; it stands with the fold perpendicular to the floor.

I simply pass out that folded note card to a group of two to three students. After students are set up, standing facing the folded card, I call out "Heads!" "Shoulders!" "Knees!" or "Toes!" I do it randomly to get students moving as they place their hands on the body part that is announced. Watch videos on how it's played.

Then I say "Cup!" The first person to grab the notecard (i.e., the cup) gets a point. Students often jump up from excitement from winning or losing. I play the game to five. The game reaffirms that body movement brings good energy and spirit for learning, an energizing way to start class or provide a mid-class break.

Humor Creates Unity

Some people, while physically fit, are a snore to be with, saying "Plank you" instead of "Thank you." Perhaps they lost touch with that great ab workout: laughing your ass off.

So, with the premise that learning requires energy, we must ask to what end? Ultimately, we need to create a feeling of "We are in it together." "I care about you." "We can learn from each other."

A speedy way to open the heart is by creating a chuckle. Laughter reveals our inherent musicality as a species. It's the sound of people responding to each other in time, intensity, and (perhaps) pitch. Create a rhythm in your setup, punchline, and laughter — do that with some predictability by reading from a joke book for 5-year-olds — and you're creating music.

I'm talking knock-knock and dad jokes. The more infantile, the better. Create a symphonic experience of call and response. Do so to create a feeling of belonging.

Hint: Buy a joke book for young children. Perhaps you're concerned: "These dumbass jokes will make me look like one." Remember your competition: your colleagues. Are they beginning class with knock-knock jokes?

It'll get ridiculous. You'll say, "Knock, knock." And then you'll respond to your own setup: "Who cares!" because you're having fun. You're creating humdingers.

Do it for a minute.

Of course, obviously, duh, uh ... hell yes, dear reader. Get your students to tell jokes, too.

Taking yourself too seriously is a surefire way to drown. A sense of humor is a life preserver.

Activity: Make a New Friend

I once taught a class that was toxically cliquey, where students looked at each other suspiciously at all times. For whatever reason, personality clashes erupted. I got frustrated. This led me to lecture the class. Translation: I created my own "new crazy" saying something to the effect of "WTF?" But that gave me the impetus the next day to do something new.

Once the bell rang, I randomly asked students to talk to each other for at least five minutes, especially those who were not sociable with each other. For example, I might ask a "stoner" to talk to an "overachiever," or an extrovert to talk to the introvert. I said, "Sit on a desk. Talk to each other for five minutes with the goal of making a new friend."

I wrote a question on the board to stoke the conversation. Here are some examples:

- What was the best thing that happened to you this year? What was so good about it? Why did it happen? What can you do to make sure it happens again?

- Of all places in the world, where would you want to live? Why?
- What's more important to you, sports or art? What does one get that the other doesn't? Is there something that one can learn from the other?

The only rule: Do not share with me or anyone what you spoke about with your new friend. Make it a private conversation.

I monitored them talking to each other to make sure no one student dominated. They needed to show an interest in each other.

We did that every day for a week. Afterward, we did the "make a new friend" activity once a week. Over time, the cliques broke away. Students grew more comfortable with each other. Class-wide conversations grew spontaneous and engaging. Class became more memorable.

I love the expression, "Democracy in the Classroom." Feels like Horace Mann would have said such a thing. It happens when we value each person, when everyone's experiences are heard, and when each person is taken seriously.

"Make a New Friend" has helped me set the groundwork for all students to be heard, even in my most cliquey classes. While never a perfect solution (what is?), it's a good start.

What I've described above is how I approach the first minute or two of class.

It's my way of saying, "Welcome."

But teaching in our disruptive new normal requires more than knock-knock jokes. It is a victory to start class with a smile, but jokes don't prevent shipwrecks.

Below I explain my vision for teaching — my map and rudder through today's storms.

My Vision for Teaching

My goal is to *help students use what they've learned to make something new so that they can clearly communicate their insights about the world.* In doing so, I have five pillars that I rely upon: 1) connecting to the world, 2) radical humility, 3) failing forward, 4) learning publicly, and 5) teaching from the back of the classroom, which I describe in the next section.

Connecting to the world: Perhaps you've heard of the butterfly effect. It's the idea coined by mathematician Edward Lorenz, who said that microscopic random acts can have unpredictable outsize consequences on the future. For example, when a butterfly flaps its wings in Brazil, it can cause a tornado in Texas. It describes the interconnectedness of all things — ecosystems, planets, and stars to you and me. The butterfly effect also asks us to see beyond the denotative meaning of things, because a butterfly is not just a butterfly. It's a metaphor to stoke feelings of awe and to embolden us to learn more about our world.

So, I think of course content as a (broken) lens in a periscope through which to see our world. This is not easy, but it's my North Star. When we ask big questions and stoke conversations, and when we understand our course content beyond the denotative and explicit meaning of a curriculum, a classroom can come to life.

From your small pocket of lint, a sense of wonder about the universe can begin, if we let it. Wonder is in the numeracy, the test tubes, the words, the pixels, the clay, the art, the music, and the games we employ. Even our little pinkie finger that moves on command is magisterial.

When our students are so inspired to make those connections, and when we are bold enough to give students the helm, the chaos abates. Because wonder moves our "ship of class" instead of a memorized answer, our ship may well sink. Fantastic. We get a brand-new ship tomorrow.

Radical humility: Radical humility is a core assumption. I know nothing. The world constantly changes. Perceptions are flawed. Vocabulary and grammar confuse me. Eyes can't see everything. And we often fool ourselves that all we see is all there is. This is the broken lens through which we see the world.

So, we need radical humility. Once we realize we are small and the universe is impossibly large, the journey can begin.

We need humility because math, science, language, art, or any discipline is dynamic, new, and *now* — and incomplete. One plus one is endlessly complex. Binary codes comprise AI algorithms. But they are too complex for anyone to understand (just 1s and 0s, people). So asking big questions with no established answer is crucial, so I must also learn alongside my students.

Radical humility also gives us permission to say with our students, "I don't know. Let's find out."

If you are more interested in how I ask questions to stoke curiosity, see Appendix I, where there's a copy of my article in the *NJEA Review*, "What Would X say?"

Failure is the way: It is crucial for students to be provided space to fall on their faces in front of friends and with meaningful feedback try again. As I see it, learning is a process of growing from mistakes. We need to know where we failed. It's gold.

I am not talking about students rewriting essays. Neither am I describing students retaking tests. Those may be excellent practices. I'm talking about something more fundamental. Because the world is complex, because knowledge is fleeting, and because course content is a broken lens through which to see the world, mistakes become an essential step in the process of meaningful understanding.

To summarize my approach in a sentence: "When the bar is high and the stakes are low, good things happen."

"When the bar is high" refers to our efforts to understand the world.

"The stakes are low" means acknowledging from the get-go that we will fall short in fully understanding the world. But we always try.

That's when "good things happen." When we embrace mistakes as robust opportunities to learn — when students are given permission to speak imperfectly or awkwardly and then with practice, kick butt — it's amazing. Students come to understand that learning is a process that requires grit, teamwork, empathy, and communication skills. A sense of humor also makes the journey better.

Fall on your face in front of your friends: And finally there is the question, how do we get students to do something difficult, to fail and try again? My answer is for students to fail in front of their friends.

Learning often needs to be public. This way students have skin in the game. Peers gain motivation to help each other improve. Trying again is celebrated. Feelings of empathy increase. And students come to realize, "We are in it together." This leads to high fives as feelings of accomplishment emerge. Failing publicly also creates a culture of growth and inclusivity. In my view, if I'm not providing students with robust opportunities to make mistakes publicly and try again with the help of community in some capacity, I am missing the mark for creating the kind of classroom that keeps me inspired to keep teaching — and probably for students to be inspired to try again.

This is one of the reasons sports and dramatic arts are so compelling. They allow us to watch athletes or artists respond to pressure, overcome setbacks, and demonstrate excellence and teamwork, because they are demonstrating the kind of resilience we expect from ourselves.

But especially with the rise of AI, failing in front of (or with) your peers in the classroom has added significance. AI's use is predicated on asking *it* for answers. But let's not deny ourselves that pleasure. We can tap into our unlimited potential when we ask ourselves "impossible" questions and have the gall to find out. Not our successes, but rather our responses to failure with the help of classmates represents the best of the human spirit. We see this in our classrooms. It's the mistakes and trying again that show our humanity because of a) the recognition of the mistake, b) the love and support from community in the face of setbacks, and c) the courage to try again to improve. Adversity brings us together. Surely, AI will help us, but it must always be leveraged to cultivate grit in the classroom.

I do this in two ways: by assigning 1) "impossible" speeches and 2) "impossible" tests.

"Impossible" speeches: Most people fear public speaking (I suspect) because they're given only one chance to deliver their speech. This understandably leads to self-consciousness and stammering. But if we can change the paradigm from "one-and-done" to "try again in community," the most frightening act — public speaking — can become an empowering one.

In my class, when students are asked to deliver two-minute speeches with no notes, they know it will be difficult. But they also know they'll have at least one more opportunity to hit it out of the park. So, they're more open to making mistakes. Students come to rely on each other for help. And when they try again, they often experience growth and a feeling of empowerment, because they have learned not only from their own, but also everyone else's mistakes. (This approach is described in detail in Appendix II, where you can find my article published in the *NJEA Review,* "Two Minutes to Mastery: Climbing the Mountain of Public Speaking.") More on his later.

Another way that I do this is by assigning "**Impossible" tests.**

In short, students are given a very difficult "test" at the beginning of a unit. They take it at least twice. The first time, students take the "impossible" test together to teach each other the material. They get an answer key at the end of the period. This is graded for five points.

The second time students take the same test alone the next day. This is graded for ten points. The big idea is that students can retake the test as many times as needed to ace it. This gives them opportunities to make mistakes and to try again.

Before you call me insane, remember, the test basically counts for nothing (only five or ten points). But it provides opportunities to master basic information, which is then used to generate interesting conversations, essays, or projects. This is discussed in greater detail in Appendix III, where you'll find my article in the *NJEA Review,* "Let's Reinvent Testing."

And me? I'm in the back of the classroom watching students help each other. This has made my job less stressful and more rewarding. By admitting their vulnerability, e.g., hearing students say, "I need help with this..." and seeing other students help each other, the growth begins.

Also, their second and third chances to try again in community encourages students to surpass their perceived limits.

Low stakes are an invitation for all of us to slow down.

A high bar leads us to unite to master difficult tasks.

Failing publicly is an invitation for us to ask for help. And trying again is our chance to fly, butterfly.

Tools for an Optimal Learning Space

You need to know what's in my classroom to appreciate my rituals. They make a difference.

1. I have a **wireless microphone and amplifier.** The microphone allows me to be a gentle conductor of a cacophonous orchestra; my classroom tends to be noisy. No need to scream, the amplifier allows me to talk calmly. Everyone can hear it, which allows for a higher level of intensity in the classroom and easier classroom management. (Yes, I bought the microphone and amplifier with my own money.)

2. **Computer monitor in the back of the classroom.** In the back of my classroom, I have a standing desk. On top of that sits a 25-inch computer screen. This setup allows me to make the classroom more amenable to physical movement. It allows me and the students to talk one-on-one or in small groups in the back of the classroom.

3. **Students' desks and chairs.** All classrooms have desks and chairs that are not connected to each other. This allows us to engage in our

frequent morning ritual: Sit on the desk and face toward the back of the room.

4. Finally, and this is crucial for me, my laptop has **screen annotation software** ZoomIt. It allows me to draw arrows, circles, and squares in different colors on any screen at any time. Also, I can set timers and zoom into (i.e., magnify) a segment of the screen, like onto a map or picture. ZoomIt is like a high-tech pointer for presentations. Get some kind of on-screen annotation software.

Experiment: Teach from the Back of the Class

As much as possible, I teach from the back of the classroom.

Teaching in chaotic times is made more difficult by teaching from the front of the classroom for these reasons: It requires unsustainable expenditures of energy for teachers and students. It hinders getting good data from students. It puts teachers at risk of putting their foot in their mouth, as they're doing most of the talking. It makes classroom management a pain in the ass. Also, it makes helping students one-on-one impossible while you lecture. It also can make everyone restless — including you.

Here's an idea: can you rethink your craft by teaching from the back of the classroom? Can you inspire students to work together where they are front and center?

This is a thought experiment, not a magic bullet. Consider the power of your course content to inspire games, skits, presentations, debates, speeches, songs, art, or creating chatbots, computer programs, simulations, and/or conversations.

I get it. Algebra is not the most debatable topic. But didn't Galileo say that the universe is written in the language of mathematics? Can't we get students to see just a glint of the majesty of the universe through math or whatever you teach?

For me, when *students* are front and center, I'm teaching better. It's more manageable and in the end more effective. When students focus on their thoughts and insights with each other, that's a good place for all of us to be.

Experiment with New Techniques: The Results May Surprise You

For the past twelve years, I've used the following techniques to teach from the back of the classroom. Steal what works.

1. Video lectures work better than lecturing from the front of the room.

2. Via a system of "collaborative testing," have students teach each other the material.
3. The next day, students retake the same test individually.
4. Students then answer big questions that connect course content to the world.

Video lecture: Instead of watching me lecture from the front of the classroom, my students take notes on video lectures and readings that I created or curated. Students begin a unit by having at least two uninterrupted days to work individually. Generally most students (85%+) prefer working individually by taking notes on video lectures and readings. Others may prefer one-on-one instruction with me; we would do that in the back of the classroom.

As students work at their own pace, they can better self-advocate for what they don't understand because they can stop the video, get up from their desk, and talk to me one-on-one — or a classmate. Also, they can "rewind" something they missed. The pressure is not on me (or even the students) to understand things perfectly the first time through, because they have the time to read, watch, and reflect on what they're learning. Also, my videos are highly edited so I can explain things as clearly as possible in the shortest amount of time. This has resulted in a class that is laid-back, focused, and structured.

Collaborative testing, Part I: After the two days of independent work on videos and reading, students take an "impossible" test collaboratively. It's open-note and generally comprises between 100 to 200 questions of all kinds: multiple correct, matching, fill in the blank, chronology, etc. Students have only one class period to complete it. It is worth only five points (low stakes). The test is difficult by design (a high bar). Students get a grade and answer key once they submit their answers at the end of the period (instant computer-generated feedback and awareness of mistakes).

When students work on the tests together, they learn better than by my lecturing from the front of the classroom. Because they are the ones teaching and arguing their way through the material, they are the ones becoming fluent with the vocabulary, concepts, and insights. They are the ones holding each other accountable for knowing the material.

Tests can be retaken after school with unlimited opportunities to try again. The best grade goes in the grade book.

One more thing: I have seen epic conversations among students while they take the test together. Generally, they're too engaged in it to require my attention.

Collaborative testing, Part II: The next day, students retake the same test. This time, it's taken individually, with no notes, only once, and it's worth only ten points (again, low stakes). They may also retake the individual test after school to improve their grade. Unlimited attempts.

I want everyone to earn a 100 on this "impossible" test, because students' fluency with course material will be required for the next phase, the Project Phase. In fact, most students earn over a 95% on these difficult tests because of the instant feedback and the opportunities to retake. Additionally, students want to show each other — and themselves — that they know the material; this is evidenced by their willingness to help each other succeed. (Also, the online test-taking software I use tracks how long students study at home for their test, which is about an hour or so for most students, which means to me, they're working hard and experiencing success because of it.)

In an end-of-year survey of 2022-23, with 96 students responding, 96.9% said that doing the test twice is a good idea. In another survey in 2023, with 88 students responding, 98% of them said that taking the test twice was worthwhile.

I like the fact that students' fluency with course material allows them to engage in high-level conversations in the Project Phase. Also, it's rather amazing that these very low-stakes assignments (five points for a collaborative quiz and ten points for the individual attempt) spur so much student energy and interest.

Project phase: In the final phase (worth 50 to 100 points), students make something new with what they learned, often to help improve their understanding about the world. How they do this can vary. Students may deliver a two-minute speech with no notes. They may participate in a debate, create a video, write an essay, or perform in a skit. There are many ways up "Project Mountain." I want students to teach their peers and feel seen and heard.

Finally, I frequently reflect on my pedagogy. Am I hitting the marks? Is class challenging and welcoming? Can students make mistakes and help each other try again? Over the course of the last ten years, based on student survey results, the answer is yes but not for reasons that were clear to me. Survey results indicated that what students liked was that they could exercise in the beginning of class, share a joke, or get into deep conversations.

I thought I was bringing rigor, but my students valued the punchlines. This is a bit counterintuitive but not necessarily contradictory. Throughout the years, students have regularly produced excellent test scores (they know the material) and they have often delivered thoughtful two-minute speeches without notes, and sometimes have written beautifully.

But they remember the knock-knock jokes.

Teaching from the back of the classroom has reconfigured my role from authoritarian to joyful instigator. The lower stress for everyone has apparently made class laid-back yet rigorous.

One More Thought Experiment: The Topic Isn't Interesting. You're Interesting.

Your students are far more interesting than you or anything you teach. This insight came from a nightmare in 2006 when my school first issued laptop computers to each student.

I was teaching The Treaty of Versailles, the calamitous "peace treaty" signed after World War I that laid the groundwork for Nazi Germany, chaos in the Middle East, and nearly destroyed my career. There I stood in 2006 in the front of my class, lecturing on the infamy of the Treaty of Versailles, not realizing I was creating my own.

As I spoke, students surfed on ESPN or YouTube on their brand-new school-issued laptops. There they sat at their desks facing me, with their computer screens facing toward the back of the room, away from me. I thought traditional methods could work because I was not yet familiar with how to teach with laptop computers. It was a disaster.

I gave everything to get students' attention. I gestured like a Broadway performer. I changed my cadence like a yodeler. I asked questions like a comedian. I grew frustrated, depressed, and despondent. I perseverated over quitting. I actually spoke to the principal about it at the time. I had created a Treaty of Versailles in my classroom by teaching a lesson about it.

Computer: 1.

Coleman: 0.

What I didn't understand — and it was right in front of me — was that YouTube was more interesting than I was. With their screens facing away from me, we were literally on different pages. I had to invent a new method to teach. So I went back to graduate school to answer the question: How do I teach with laptops? A lot of what I learned from that research is in the book you're now reading.

One of the takeaways was this: The most interesting thing in the world is you.

If I could redirect the conversation from YouTube to you, or from the denotative math-or-science curriculum (whatever course you teach) to include you, then maybe I could break the spell of the computer screen. Maybe I could get students interested in what they thought as opposed to scrolling for viral videos.

Furthermore, if I could leverage computer technology to expedite meaningful research, maybe I could create a shared conversation about the world. By students being an audience to each others' thoughts, maybe their focus could shift from their screens to their classmates and themselves.

What is interesting about asking that simple question, "What do you think?" and answering it publicly is that we learn about the importance of revision. When you listen to someone intently, speakers tend to think more carefully about what they are saying. Furthermore, because most young people have not had the experience of being heard or taken seriously, they'll tend to research and speak more deliberately. That moment of realization — I am being heard — is priceless. (This also goes for me as a teacher. I need to rephrase things all the time because I am not a smooth speaker; I'm quite a flawed one.)

The point is, listening is a superpower. Trust results when we value imperfections (because perfectionism is kryptonite). A universe of possibility appears as we go deeper into the simple question, "What do you think?"

On Possible B.S. and … Hypocrisy

I'm calling myself out on my bullshit. What I wrote above sounds magical, as in "abracadabra," put students front and center and their genius will unfurl. I said something to the effect of: Learning needs to be public so students have skin in the game … yada yada.

And now … a story to convey my hypocrisy.

I often share a classroom with my colleague and longtime friend. Let's call him Jim. He once walked into the classroom while I was teaching. Not unusual. I was at the front of the room — a problem right away — asking students what they thought was interesting. With marker in hand, I wrote their answers on the whiteboard, as we brainstormed our next project. (It was in the beginning of the school year, October 2011, when my reinvention from traditional teaching had begun. I was in the midst of writing my doctoral dissertation and would graduate in May 2012. I was still a newbie to the "new me.")

Students said these were interesting topics: Britney Spears, the LA Lakers, Call of Duty (video game), Instagram, Justin Bieber. Jim laughed privately in the back of the classroom because he knew that stuff was a snore to me.

And so I responded to students, "Why is Britney Spears interesting?"

Some students answered, "She's hot."

I responded, "But people have been hot since the big bang. Sexual attraction is as old as life itself. Give me more."

Silence.

So I crossed out Britney Spears on the board and said, "Why are the LA Lakers so interesting?"

They responded, "They have Kobe Bryant. Great player."

I retorted, "There have always been great players. Wasn't Michael Jordan a great player, or Kareem Abdul-Jabbar? What makes Kobe Bryant singularly interesting?"

They murmured, "Basically, he's clutch and works hard."

"Jordan was clutch. Sorry. Nothing unique here." I crossed out his name.

This went on for all the other topics they listed.

Jim laughed harder. He then asked from the back of the classroom, "Why did you ask students what they thought was interesting and then cross them out?"

(On a side note, in May 2023, eleven years later, I asked the same question: "What's interesting to you?" This time students made compelling arguments about Taylor Swift. [Remember, it was the end of the school year. Students knew my expectations.] Without my prompting, a number of students in different classes created PowerPoint presentations to argue, yes, Taylor Swift is an important artist. She speaks to a generation of young people, has musical sophistication, puts on a great show, and is a role model who makes her audiences feel seen and heard. Great conversations. No complaints from me. Call me a Swifty.)

But on that October day in 2012, students' answers killed me, like swallowing jagged pills. I interrupted them: "Louis XIV, Europe's longest-reigning monarch, is the most interesting person ever. He created 'Disney World' for spies — his palace at Versailles — changed fashion globally, revolutionized governance, was responsible for 50 years of war that proved consequential for Europe. Yet his (almost) dying breath was, 'I warred too much.' He was the most skilled political actor ever. He invented and played the part of king throughout his life — writing, directing, and acting the role. That dude was fascinating!"

But was I unfair? I asked students on-the-spot what they found interesting. They had no prior opportunity to research and craft their argument.

Rather, I had studied Louis XIV for the past ten years. I'd read and taught about him and had been trained to construct and deliver compelling arguments. Maybe my students were blindsided.

It's easy to think we are deeply humble when in fact we may be snobs. Jim may be right. By crossing out the names of what students found interesting, Jim says, I invalidated their interests.

But I want students to make clear and compelling arguments, immediately, succinctly, and clearly. It's a balancing act to cultivate students' curiosity. It's difficult to connect course content to the world, as difficult as seeing yourself clearly in the mirror.

Furthermore, most people have never had the opportunity to be taken seriously. Fewer still have had their interests cultivated in an academic setting where they were given permission to speak awkwardly and try again. Eloquence takes practice, failure, feedback, and friendship. So does teaching. I say this to be real. Teaching has never been easy. It's more difficult now.

Ethics of Teaching in Our Chaotic New Normal

But asking "What do you think?" also leads to a glaring ethical issue, which I have not heard addressed at scale. If, upon learning about the world, students come to the conclusion that we're screwed (*i.e.,* all is lost), then we will have failed them and our society.

Walking the line between promoting an honest appraisal of what is happening in the world while empowering them is difficult. For this reason, one of the interviewees in Part 3 chose to remain anonymous. Additionally, such a conclusion would crush everyone's mental health in the classroom.

This begs for a reframing of idealistic mission statements like those in the New Jersey Learning Standards for social studies, of fostering civic mindedness and global awareness. When mechanically implemented, they could become a recipe for a general feeling of helplessness and burnout.

This is revealed in a new diagnosis in the field of mental health, *solastalgia.* It refers to the psychological upheaval that results from individuals whose lives have been disrupted by ecological disasters, or who have felt powerless in how to respond to bearing witness to sudden environmental catastrophes.

I could only imagine how distressing it must be for many young people who see news of an impending apocalypse from all directions, 24/7. How could this make anyone, let alone a young person, feel engaged to learn about the world? And how does one teach about it? "What's the point?" could be an honest answer to an earnest question to compel "civic mindedness and global awareness."

So we need to face this ethical quandary: How do we connect our courses to the world when learning about it could be traumatizing? And what is the cost to society if we ignore such issues?

I have ideas, but they are inadequate. We need a colloquium, not a sound bite. What follows is a brainstorm to help us teach through our chaotic new normal.

First, we must answer this question: Does the news (*i.e.,* studying a societal problem) help us better understand course content? For example, the disaster at the nuclear reactor at Fukushima in 2011 showed footage of tsunamis wiping out villages in seconds. Horrifying. What would be the point of showing such footage to a classroom? Does it help us better understand course content or the world? In 2011 I taught U.S. history. In that instance, I would say no it did not. Yes it gave rise to larger issues of sustainable energy, but that connection was too much of a stretch, given what I was teaching. The deeply horrifying images would have overwhelmed any historical context.

Alternatively, would bringing up enormously controversial topics, such as the January 6th raid on the capitol, help students better understand course material? It's politically loaded. But perhaps it could help us better understand history. Perhaps it could lead to productive conversations when addressed with the highest levels of judiciousness. (But at what point does "the highest levels of judiciousness" become like "walking on eggshells?")

For example, in 2021-22, my students wrestled with this question: "How would Enlightenment thinkers have responded to the January 6th raid on the capitol?" Students were invited to research specific aspects of the raid that they found interesting; also, they were encouraged to connect their findings to the history of the Enlightenment. In short, students were asked to use what they learned about the Enlightenment to help them make sense of today's world.

With 91 students responding, 81% said they thought connecting Enlightenment ideals to better understand the January 6th raid was a meaningful experience; 91% said they felt free to research the topics they found interesting. There were no parental complaints. The unit brought a high level of engagement, as I witnessed. But my survey results were not perfect. Rather, looking back three years later, I feel a bit queasy about the whole thing, as I'll describe below.

I now feel more tentative about what current events I address in class. Today, social media makes many conspiracies go mainstream. Also, accurate news can be perfectly depressing.

We don't want students fighting with their parents or each other. We don't want to unearth topics that lead to catastrophic thinking. But if we can't address big issues in the classroom, where else could students practice the art of conversations to promote civics and democracy?

Also, I don't want to find myself depressed. But looming crises seem to bring me there: the presidential election, the wars in Ukraine and the Middle East, the growing ecological chaos from global warming. They are enough to make me eat a Happy Meal®.

We need a nationwide conversation about the ethics of teaching in our chaotic new normal.

Go Local. Go Small. Make Connections

Given those difficulties, I'm rethinking my assumptions.

In the past, I've asked students to connect course content to big issues, such as unrest in Venezuela, Trump's impeachments, AI's disruptive impact, and social media's corrosive effects. For twenty years, those issues ignited high student engagement and meaningful learning. But as we enter the new crazy, we need to rethink what it means to connect the classroom to the world. My working answer is this: Go local. Go small. Microscopic specificity is today's North Star.

In our perilous new normal, we need deep connections with our neighbors, local leaders, and local businesses — *i.e.,* our local community — far more than we need abstract explanations. This is one of my epiphanies in writing this book: Our neighborhood is an untapped resource. By going local, we sidestep the algorithms that have made our national conversations so toxic. And as students strengthen their interpersonal communication skills by having such conversations, our courses grow in relevance and engagement. Creating effective conversation will always be a crucial skill, even in an age dominated by AI.

I'm brainstorming here, but perhaps we can enlighten students on the lives of their neighbors who use math, history, science, language, or art (whatever you teach) to navigate their way through their lives.

So, here are some working revisions of old prompts through a post-June 8, 2023, lens.

Old Prompts **Before** the Sky Turned Orange, June 8, 2023.	**New** Revised Prompts **After** the Sky Turned Orange, June 8, 2023.
Are we living in a renaissance today? Compare Renaissance artwork in Europe in the 1400–1500s to a work of art today, something between 2000–2023.	*Interview a local artist, musician, writer, actor, or content creator for at least 30 minutes. Ask them: "Are we in a renaissance?" "What is the state of art today?" "What are today's masterpieces?"*
How have modern dictators taken the French Revolution (i.e., Robespierre, Murat, or Napoleon) to a new level?	*Interview a neighbor or a family member who lived under a dictatorship. Report on what you learned.*

How might AI impact the trajectory of the Industrial Revolution? Why should we care?	Interview a local business owner about what the growth of AI means to them? What are their hopes and fears? Do they see opportunities or difficulties? Why?

Last year, I asked students: *Are we living in a renaissance? Compare two works of art: one from the Renaissance in Europe to a work of art today.*

Students chose the art that interested them. They researched and then delivered two-minute speeches with no notes.

Post–June 8, 2023, that project feels cold. It makes the art seem impersonal and distant. Why not reframe the question to create a conversation with someone in their community? Brainstorming here:

Interview a local artist, musician, writer, actor, or content creator for at least 30 minutes. Ask them: "Are we in a renaissance?" "What is the state of art today?" "What are today's masterpieces?" After the interview, conduct your own research to fact-check, substantiate, and expand upon the points that were raised.

I suspect interviewing a local artist could make students' inquiry more meaningful. Art would no longer feel distant like the Sistine Chapel. Rather, we could appreciate art through our neighbor's eyes, as well as our own.

Finally, as students present their findings to the class, I predict conversation would get "meta" real quick. Students would have conversations (class discussion) about conversations (interviews) about conversations (against their own personal reflections, research, and fact-checking), which is what scholarship is: high-level conversation among informed peers who are trying to answer a challenging question.

While studying the French Revolution, I asked students, *How have modern dictators taken the French Revolution to a new level?*

Again, students delivered a two-minute speech with no notes. What resulted were thoughtful speeches that compared dictators of the 20th century to leaders during the French Revolution, such as Robespierre, Marat, or Napoleon.

Students reported in surveys that they found the project engaging. Speeches were informed and at times inspiring. The assignment also brought a feeling of teamwork as students helped each other improve.

But post-June 8, 2023, a better prompt would be, *Interview a neighbor or a family member who lived under a dictatorship. Report on what you learned.* Why should the topic of tyranny only be known through YouTube? Why not explore the history that family members or neighbors have lived through?

While not every community is composed of individuals fleeing persecution, my brainstorm may still have merit. Perhaps students could Zoom with such people and by doing so create a more intimate understanding of the history. It would raise big questions: What does it mean to have good government? Why might a dictator be a desirable or horrifying alternative for citizens — or both!

To further promote critical thinking, students would research beyond the interviewee's claims: fact-check, substantiate, and deepen their understanding of the history's connection to the interviewee.

Class discussion would take on a whole new meaning when it involves their community. It would uphold school's vital role as a safe space for inquiry, for students to stop and process what has been discussed during their interview, to further research and come to their own conclusions, and to discuss them with classmates.

Finally, I asked, *How might AI impact the trajectory of The Industrial Revolution?*

Students researched AI's impact on industries that they found interesting (e.g., automotive, communication, retail, music, etc.). They were engaged, but the conversation got dark quickly. After a student's speech, another student said, "Dr. Coleman, we're fucked." Everything stopped. Everyone turned toward her. Speechless. (Not that I disagreed. But that comment was enough to make me write a book about it.)

So, let's do better.

Why discuss AI in the abstract? Instead we could interview local businesses about what the growth of AI means to them? Admittedly, an interviewee could be uninformed, but that's why we research beyond what anyone says, fact-check, and read from various credible sources. This would also prepare students to converse with those who hold a range of views. By focusing on a small, manageable microcosm, we can better sidestep the big nationwide storm of fear and conspiracy.

Call the Number, Grab the Life Preserver

It's September 21. I am on my third edit. Nearly done. I'm interviewing friends and colleagues for Part III of this book. But I'm sick. Tonight is Back to School. Parents come to school in the evening to learn about the courses their children take. Generally speaking, it's a lovely night, a win-win-win. It's a night where everyone wants to see teachers succeed. The parents are excited to meet the teachers. The administration wants to present an appearance of the school being a great place for young people to learn. And teachers are prepared to reassure parents that "It's going to be a great year."

But I can't do it. I've done Back to School for twenty-six years straight, and this will be the first time I won't. I am sick. For the past week, I've been battling a serious cold. Congestion has built up. It's kept me awake at all hours of the night. A sore throat is killing me. The night before, I went to a doctor who prescribed antibiotics. He said I had a massive sinus infection and gave me a doctor's note that said don't go to work for the next two days.

What's kept me in the game of teaching are the conversations I've had with students about the world. But it takes tremendous effort to get there. Students do a lot of research. (I do a lot of research!) And I put myself out there. I make mistakes constantly. I prove daily that you can fly and get shot down simultaneously.

And so a new year has begun. Again I've begun brainstorming on how to connect course content to the world. But it is getting me depressed. This is the same course I've taught for the past 26 years. The world changes, so projects change. So, I learn deeply about what's happening in the world now. I feel anxious. I sense the disregard that some students have ("Why know about Afghanistan?"), I perseverate while reviewing sources. I feel stuck. What are students going to *do* with this? Write an essay? (Ugh, grading essays is hell.) Deliver a speech or debate? (Great but so time-consuming.) Does anyone care?

It so happens, as we are learning about Afghanistan, the U.S. military has suddenly withdrawn after more than a 20-year presence there. This has led to an instantaneous collapse of that society, a sudden U-turn in their history from educating young women to putting them back in their houses like prisoners who fear for their safety. I feel a whiplash. I think about that poor man who hung onto the last plane to leave Kabul, who fell 1,000 feet to his death as he tried to escape.

And just recently, I heard from retired General Petraeus on a podcast. He said if the United States had kept only 3,000 troops in Afghanistan, the country would've been saved. Women would continue to be educated. The nation would be stable. But that's not what happened. We know what happened. It fell to the Taliban as if nothing had happened for the past 20 years with the U.S. presence. All that violence, all that trauma, treasure, tragedy. For what?

I am veering from what I promised myself. My morning ice bath, exercise, and sunlight are not helping. It weighs me down, the work I'm about to engage in for the next ten months. Many nights and weekends will be sacrificed grading papers, lesson planning, or researching the next big question. Maybe it's not worth it. Maybe I'm creating a Treaty of Versailles in my mind.

So on the morning of Back to School, I called that number, the one that arranges for a substitute teacher.

I took the day off.

No students. I emailed them my lesson plans. No parents. I emailed them a video that I created earlier in the year to introduce myself to them. I concluded my email to both parents and students, "If you have any questions, please reach out." And then I went back to bed and slept for the next three hours.

Later in the day I spoke to my friend Charleen, whom I interviewed in Part III. She said, "You sound sick." She followed up, "Isn't our goal this year to slow down?" We speak on the phone quite often about teaching.

I'm writing this now, because Charleen told me to. She said, "If you're writing about teaching in The new crazy, you gotta write about what you do when it hits you."

I said, "I take a day off to put myself back together. Sometimes I grade papers. Sometimes I lesson-plan. Sometimes I go to Asbury Park, where there's a dog park on the beach." (It's one of the few places where tons of people hang out casually. The dogs bring levity. The sound of the waves and the salty air inspire me. The people are welcoming. It's a two-hour drive from home. But it's heaven.)

As teachers, we have a get-out-of-jail card. We can call somebody, who will then call somebody to take over our class for the day.

When you feel like you can't go on, call that number.

When the work overwhelms you because of grading papers, which is one of the most god-awful things anybody can do — absolute drudgery — don't suffer. Call that number.

When you're a rock star, when the kids love your class, and when you're getting no flack, call that number.

To teach in our chaotic new normal, we need more than a rudder. We also need wind to bring us to good places. With no wind, we'll be lost at sea.

But ain't it amazing what a day makes?

Later that afternoon, I made one more phone call to a friend/teacher whom I also interviewed, Lauren. I told her how I felt, and she said, "Oh, you have that beginning-of-the-year cold." She understood exactly the reaction when the grind is first felt.

I'm not complaining, because I have a lifeline, a phone number that allows me to get a substitute teacher. Few people have that. Privilege. My dad worked on lawns and construction sites; I worked alongside him for years. I also worked in a steel mill, a chemical waste plant, and fast food. I drove taxis, delivered pizzas, sold insurance, and (of course) worked in retail.

Teaching is better than all those jobs. It's probably the best job, in part because we can call that number.

So, call that number when you're drowning.

That's what I do to survive.

Do Your Five and Drive

There is an expression among some staff members in our school, "Do your five and drive," meaning teach your five classes, and then at 3:05 p.m., go home.

Early in my career, I left school long after 3:05 p.m. because I was overwhelmed: teaching myself the material, preparing lessons from scratch, and grading papers like a monk.

Then I came across Rafe Esquith's book, *Real Talk for Real Teachers,* a good read. Rafe was one of the most recognized teachers in U.S. history, but now his approach seems unsustainable. He arrived at school at 6:30 a.m. and left as late as 6:30 p.m. He spent his Christmas vacations and weekends working with his students on his famous Shakespearean productions.

Our chaotic new normal is asking us, how can we teach sustainably without sacrificing our health? I get it: great preparation makes for great results. But today's chaos has changed my priorities. I need to take better care of myself. I need stronger boundaries between work and home. At 3:05, I put students first. But now at 3:06, I put myself first. That clarity is reflected in "Do your five and drive."

The wisdom of that phrase became apparent to me after the January 6 raid on the capitol in 2021. During that time, our school district had moved to online home instruction to prevent the spread of COVID-19.

As a mob set upon the capitol, my wife burst into the room where I was teaching online. She cried, "Someone has been shot at the capitol! A mob is brutalizing police officers! It's taken over the Senate chamber!"

Not understanding the severity she was describing, I kept on teaching the Enlightenment (darkly hysterical).

The same thing happened on September 11, 2001. A teacher interrupted my class at 9:15 a.m. and whispered into my ear, "A plane has smashed into the World Trade Center!" I kept teaching without breaking stride.

I said indignantly, "Do you mind? I'm teaching something important!"

But as I caught wind of what was happening on January 6, 2021, my heart sank. One of my favorite former students was on the steps of the capitol waving an American flag. A photographer from a local newspaper took a picture of him with the mob, which went viral.

I know him quite well, the guy who was photographed on the capitol steps. He's smart, a graduate of an Ivy League school, a top student. He is personable, engaging, and has a great sense of humor. I love the guy. So I called him on the phone when I saw the picture of him that went viral. We spoke on the phone for three hours that night. We've had numerous conversations since then. They last hours whether on the phone, on a hike, or over dinner. I want to understand, "What were you thinking?"

But those conversations crush my ideals. What I taught him as a freshman now seems misinterpreted. No matter our mutual respect, it was like I had taught X but he learned Y. We cannot agree on anything: facts, conclusions, credible sources, interpretations of history in general. This is one reason our conversations last so long. We try to find common ground but can't. There is never yelling. We enjoy each other's company. But I am left dumbfounded and somewhat heartbroken.

I thought, maybe those people who stormed the capitol were uninformed. But my former student did not misunderstand what I explicitly taught. He recited with excellent recollection my lesson from ten years earlier on John Locke and the Declaration of Independence — ironically, the very lesson I was teaching when the mob struck the capitol in 2021. I thought I was teaching a lesson on critical thinking. He interpreted my lesson as a proclamation: *Liberty must be preserved!*

He said, "We are in a post-constitution age."

I said, "What would replace our constitution? How would it get ratified? Would it be a democratic process?"

Slowly it dawned on me over the course of weeks that if he has such views, so do many of my other students.

To teach in our chaotic new normal is to recognize that not everyone feels vertigo or alarm. Ground zero may well be health insurance. I teach for my livelihood, not my life. It's recognizing that my best lesson could be a seed for radicalization in a way I can't fathom.

Getting through the day, keeping the job while doing your best to inspire your students without losing your head, is a mighty achievement. This requires perspective. The world is larger than anyone's ability to comprehend.

How ironic that Rafe Esquith, the National Teacher of the Year, found himself in his own storm. Shortly after writing *Real Talk for Real Teachers*, he was fired for allegedly telling "an improper joke to students and inappropriately touching minors."[15] This resulted in his being hospitalized from stress. Very. Disturbing. Stuff. Whether or not the charges are true (his lawsuit resulted in a settlement), my point is that today such allegations are easier to make, go viral, and destroy people's lives.

So, professional boundaries are essential. At 3:05 p.m. I'm done teaching, or at least I try to be. I must take care of myself, my family, and my dear friends. I must accept my limitations. And I must accept that no matter how earnestly I try to communicate anything, it could be misinterpreted by even my best student.

"Do your five and drive" also reveals that loving your neighbors can feel impossible. That's why as a good sucker, you need faith in people's ability to reason. My former student and I still talk regularly, play guitar, and I'll see him at a gig occasionally. We will never cancel each other or understand each other. We meet to say to ourselves that we are more than our differences. Our respect is too deep and yet our understanding is too elusive. I guess conversation can only do so much. A question —"?"— has only so much power.

---

[15] Twitter, et al. "Rafe Esquith Fired: Former Teacher of the Year Accused of Inappropriately Touching Minors." *Los Angeles Times*, 15 Oct. 2015, www.latimes.com/local/education/la-me-esquith-20151015-story.html. Accessed 3 Apr. 2024.

Part of our work-life balance can be found in evening routines. That balance starts when we have a clear boundary as implied by "Do your five and drive."

I didn't before January 6, 2021. But now I do.

Additional Routines to Even the Keel

I started writing this book once the 2022-23 school year ended. It is intended as a letter to you and me. I committed myself to writing six days a week, an hour each day, and figured that by the end of the summer this book would be complete. By August 23, I completed my first draft.

During my morning writing sessions, I was little reminded of the toxic effects of digital technology because writing is so enjoyable. I noticed how psychologically healthy I felt. The prolonged focus felt like I had taken my mind to the gym.

But by around 3 p.m., temptations would percolate for me to get back on the laptop to check social media, YouTube, or Google News, and they ensnared me. I might go online to learn about X but clickbait would then hook my attention to the alphabet, causing me to forget the very reason I went online. By 7 p.m. or so, I would feel lobotomized.

So, these measures have helped me maintain my mental health:

1. I bought a Kindle Scribe, a large e-reader that allows me to read more easily. I make the font huge. I read to my heart's content. It's given me a lovely stimulant: reading without distraction. In other words, by turning off laptops and phones by 8 p.m., I'm happier and more even keeled.

2. I've taken cold showers to a new level. I bought an ice bath for $900. It allows me to plunge into 40° water. I go in for two to three minutes, doing so upon waking up and in the afternoon. Because the ice bath is so cold, my survival strategy is to breathe *deepllllllly* and *deliberatellllly* like a forced meditation — feel my breath and turn off my "mental hamster wheel." The effects are not miraculous, but the improvement in my life has been significant: far less depression and increased energy and mental sharpness. Once school starts, it will be part of my daily practice.

3. I eat an egg or some egg whites (some protein) first thing in the morning. For most of my life, I binged at night. But upon listening to a podcast with Tim Ferriss and Andrew Huberman, I heard them mention the benefits of eating some protein immediately upon waking. This, combined with viewing morning light and exercise, has helped stave off my late-night raids on the fridge. I guess there is a clock to our eating. Starting with protein first thing in the morning seems to set my clock for eating, which now turns off earlier in the day.

4. Finally, I'm learning how to slowwwww down. The worse things get, the more crucial it becomes to savor life at a glacial speed. Celebrate the cake and your company with family and friends. Slow is zen. Now is when. Deep, mindful breaths are a start. Sometimes while in the ice bath, I'll take twenty deep, perfect, deliberate breaths and won't leave until I do so. It stills my mind and calms me down.

PART III

Conversations with Colleagues

Below are interviews with six teachers I've known during my career teaching in public school. The interviewees care deeply about the job and don't share similar political views. When interviewees said things I disagreed with, I did not "correct" or "debate" them. I amplified their view to better understand what they were saying. This process has deepened our friendship and my appreciation for our journey as teachers. These interviews also mark my intention to start a larger conversation about teaching within our profession. Learning about my colleagues' lives has emboldened me to be vulnerable with you. But again my approach points to a limitation of this book: I'm interviewing teachers I know. That alone sets up a confirmation bias on my part.

With most of the interviewees — except for Charleen — it's my first time having deep conversations with them about how to teach in today's climate.

Here are the interviewees:

Chin Chu: I have known Chin for the past fifteen years, when he began teaching at River Dell High School. Our conversations last hours, and I savor them. Time flies when talking with Chin. His experience as a trained chemist (PhD from University of Minnesota) and immigrant from China who attended an elite secondary school, and whose family endured the Cultural Revolution, is particularly poignant when considering how to teach in our disruptive new normal.

Ellen Hill: I have known Ellen for as long as I've been at River Dell. Her sense of the mission is clear and inspiring: Get students to think critically. Yet she notices the impact of our chaotic new normal on students' mental health. Ellen volunteered with the Peace Corps in Botswana. Then she attended Columbia University's Teachers College. She teaches AP Biology and served as our association's vice president. She is whip smart, delightfully witty, warm, and worldly. Her presence makes my day better.

Lauren DelPiano: Lauren is a teacher of English who has been a friend for as long as she's taught at the school, eighteen years. Her dedication was proven by her ability to reinvent her craft five years ago, something that requires tremendous research, experimentation, and self-examination. Lauren also teaches composition at Montclair State University. She believes that self-awareness needs to be seen as a means as well as an end, which is especially salient in our disruptive new normal.

Anonymous: Anonymity was necessary for this interview to be published. This person is a social studies teacher somewhere in the United States. (Not a teacher at River Dell.)

Saratheresa Bartelloni: "ST" is an art teacher, a rare creative who is technologically sophisticated with a Master's in Educational Technology. She was the lead tech trainer of our school district and also taught computer science. Presently, ST teaches pottery. She's a ferocious devotee of the ukulele and has the kind of personality that makes your heart sing. She's smart, spunky, and "sparky," with an informed perspective on the AI revolution.

Charleen Martinelli: I met Charleen more than twenty years ago at Café for Socrates, a discussion group that met weekly. Over the course of two hours we, along with ten other people, discussed big philosophical questions. Sometimes those conversations led us to a bar, where we continued talking. From those experiences, I made a dear friend in Charleen. She is jet fuel. She's a gifted teacher who twice delivered the commencement address at the school where she teaches. She has a personality that says "Lead with love!" She's also a personal coach whose advice helped inspire the writing of this book. One more thing: Charleen was "promoted" to vice principal but after a year of that returned to the classroom because she missed teaching.

Chin Chu

Glen

So what does this mean to you, "How to teach in our chaotic new normal?"

Chin

Let's talk about the past five years. My observation — I speak only from my personal experience — I see an erosion in freedom of expression. People are becoming a lot more cautious. So, I find myself more and more self-censoring. I'm staying away from perceived controversial topics.

Glen

That's interesting. If students can't explore controversial topics in the classroom, where would they? Wouldn't young people benefit from being part of a conversation with a caring, dispassionate adult — a teacher?

Chin

I'll give you an example. We're building our curriculum and have to talk about climate change. And it's fairly one directional: human activity, fossil fuels, and carbon dioxide are the big contributors.

I'm trained to be skeptical of everything, to consider other points of view by interrogating the data. I want to invite a range of points of view to invite a larger conversation to spur critical thinking.

Glen

What kind of training would prepare you to be so skeptical?

Chin

During my doctoral work, every week we had group meetings led by a P.I., a principal investigator, who was a professor. The premise was to interrogate the raw data generated by graduate students: couple of postdocs, first-year, second-year, even the fifth-year graduate students — we would all attend weekly meetings to present findings. We would all drill into the data. We would ask, "What is good data?" We learned, don't make any claim unless you have data to back it up. This training taught me that the process is rigorous. More times than not, things were missing and we were trained to look for holes in the data, the experiment, or more importantly the analysis, etc. Nobody was to take anything at face value.

Glen

Can I say that compared to most people I've come across in my teaching career, there's an argument to be made that you're academically gifted, at least talented. You attended a top-tier, highly competitive secondary school in China and graduated near the top of your class. Then you came to the United States, learned English, and got a PhD in chemistry. That's interesting to me. You're highly educated, an immigrant, and now a chemistry teacher. You have a unique perspective.

You were talking about climate change before.

Chin

Yes. It's interesting. I've been through a competitive school system and graduated near the top of my class. But looking back, especially from junior high all the way through high school years, I felt like I totally didn't fit in because I'm very curious. I'm always asking the question, "Why?" The system in China doesn't tolerate that. You could not go there. You soak up what they teach. Accept their standard answers. Memorize. Move on. No questions.

I'll give you a great example. I love history. In high school, I was interested in World War II and European history, which were not on the national entrance exam. History was not taught at all. No classes about World War II. I was so bored out of my mind. So, I went to my high school library. I dug out the books myself. While other people were doing rote stuff, I was in the library reading history. So, I never felt like I fit in their mold.

Glen
So when you hear climate change as a given orthodoxy, fossil-fuel based, you're thinking what as a scientist?

Chin
That's actually an interesting evolution for me. If you talked to me five years ago, I would've bought it wholeheartedly. It's indisputable. It's man-made. The earth is in a very bad place. I bought into the whole claim of fossil fuel, carbon dioxide, greenhouse gasses, and all that. I started to have some doubts about three or four years ago.

Glen

What caused your doubts?

Chin

I think COVID-19 really pushed me to start questioning everything more than I did before. At the very beginning, it was very scary. And then the vaccine came out. I looked at the technology. It was great. And then, wait a second ... We're doing school virtually? Then I spent more time online. I learned about the Great Barrington Declaration.

Glen

What's that?

Chin

In October of 2020, a bunch of world-renowned infectious disease experts from Stanford, Harvard, and MIT said that we should have targeted protection. I only heard about this in mid-2021, a year after we had been in lockdown, which had profound impacts on our society. So, if we targeted protection, a lot of those impacts could have been reduced.

Glen

Targeted protection? In other words, target certain populations like the elderly?

Chin

The elderly and people with comorbidities. But don't shut down the whole society. Protect the nursing homes, hospitals, and the high-risk population. The rest of society should live in a normal way. The authors of the

Barrington Declaration were viciously attacked and censored. And that's what concerns me, the total intolerance of different points of view.

Glen

Can I share something that I learned recently? I was listening to an interview with a guy who wrote for *The Wall Street Journal*. He was an editor of a big newspaper in Israel, *Haaretz* or *Jerusalem Post*. Now he writes for *The New York Times*. He said the problem with COVID-19 was that scientists had no humility. Scientists were saying, "This is the answer. Take it or leave it." And this resulted in many citizens rejecting scientific authorities.

Chin

There's one key point I want to get off my chest. The one personal quality that should be most appreciated in our society is humility. It's having the guts to say, "We got it wrong." Or, "I got it wrong." But human nature is not like that, especially for people with a certain fame or reputation. It is extraordinarily challenging for such a person to come out and humbly say, "I was wrong." Rather, people follow prevailing recommendations, which result in a hierarchy of information. Those highest have the power to turn off the volume on others. And that is worrisome.

Suddenly, my training from grad school started flooding back. I thought, "Wait a minute. I need to think a little bit harder about COVID-19 as well as climate change." If everyone is screaming X, perhaps part of the problem is that people are screaming instead of talking rationally, obsessing about X instead of thinking methodically about it.

For example, sometimes I have students doing research on eco-anxiety among teenagers. I stay away from it because I don't want to poke the hornet's nest. This is where I feel the most uncomfortable about the recent development. Divergent views get canceled. Yet science requires divergent hypotheses, insightful analysis of data, and robust conversations about them. So, I'm starting to self-censor.

If we're warming, and it seems that's the case, nature is going to happen. It's probably tropical regions that will quickly become uninhabitable. The far northern and southern parts of the globe will be more temperate. It won't be pretty. As we have for tens of thousands of years, humans will migrate. Humans have migrated before from climate change and will continue to do so.

Glen
So, the climate crisis is framed like this: We are at the precipice of a disaster. Then a smarty-pants comes along and says, "There's more to the story."

Chin
When someone says, "We're at a crisis point, a tipping point," that hysteria is also saying to the populace, "Shut up. Do what I say." That's my experience in China, where we were always in crisis mode. To me, this is the wrong direction for how we approach our conversations about

science. We need to be able to discuss and interrogate the data rationally as a society. Scientists need to educate citizens and convince them that there is a crisis. But many scientists instead treat citizens like children, which shuts down our conversation and democracy. That's what happened during COVID-19.

Rather, we need to get citizens away from crisis mode. When we can interrogate the data rationally without the hysteria, then the best ideas will come to the fore. We need to embrace that process, or we short-circuit our ability to analyze. Unfortunately, the process takes time and requires tolerance of all members in our society.

Glen

I have a response. I think climate scientists would say, "Are you a scientist? Who are you to question those who've trained throughout their lives in this specialized realm, topics that they pore over daily? Who are you, Chin Chu, to question the scientists?"

Chin

I don't need to be a trained scientist. I just need to be a human with some critical thinking. When we are not allowed to start saying "Wait a minute," then we are not allowing the citizenry to think for themselves. George Carlin had a great bit about that: The earth will be fine. It's we who are in trouble. My point is, provide a space where a range of views can be heard so that we can interrogate assumptions and the data. That's what scientific thinking is about.

Glen

Couldn't you teach this by having students read journal articles from *Nature* [one of the most reputable journals of science] or other vaunted publications? This way they can read the article and then people can make their own decisions?

Chin

The problem is that science is getting highly politicized. We saw this with COVID-19. We were told that society must shut down, and this negatively impacted our students. Florida refused to do so and yet their COVID-19 rates were the same as those areas that were locked down. *Nature's* editorials genuinely concern me. They are getting involved in political debates.

Glen

My eco-anxiety is not caused by what's happening with the ecology alone. It's also caused by our failure to talk about science intelligently as a society. Once you get called out on the carpet as a teacher — once, twice, three times — you're out. The process will exhaust you. Most of us will start to say it is not worth it to teach big questions. Most will get anxious at the thought of saying something "taboo," even if it is in the interest of cultivating scholarly conversations. Too risky for most people and yet too critical to ignore.

Chin

Yeah, this is what I worry about the most. The general academic environment is not healthy. We can't just sit down and talk. It's scary. It's as if the Cultural Revolution is coming to the USA now.

Glen
The Cultural Revolution? How does that connect?

Chin
Yeah, I didn't personally experience the Cultural Revolution. I was too young. I was born toward the end. But my parents did.

Glen
And they told you about it?

Chin
Very reluctantly. They were lucky to survive. My mom told me she went to an engineering school in the 1950s. The government said to everyone, "Citizens, tell us what we can do better. We're open for constructive criticism." It was a trap! A lot of the people who made "helpful" suggestions were sent to "reeducation" camps. It triggers me. Mentioning reeducation triggers me. That's what my parents' generation went through. My mom only survived because she was interning in a factory in a remote region. So she was not participating in the tumult. That was the only reason she survived.

Glen
Wasn't that the Hundred Flowers Campaign, or something like that?

Chin

Yeah. The government was "open." The government was so "honest" only to find out who was disloyal. It's history. It's the purge. Russia is no different. Dictatorships are no different. One of the books I read floored me: *1984*. It's that part of "permitted thoughts."

Glen

We want healthy conversations where different views can be expressed, even if views of some students are unpopular. That's how democracy works. Yes?

Chin

We need to have open and honest discussions, especially about science. Put evidence on the table and look at what would be the best solution. Ask ourselves, "What is good data and the proper analysis?" It cannot be, "This is the singular solution and no conversation. No questions." We need a space where divergent ideas can be explored.

Glen

But what if the majority of Americans cannot understand the science because science is generally difficult to understand to begin with. It requires an attention span, solid math skills. So maybe a national conversation isn't crucial because the subject matter is too complicated?

Chin

Lately I've started thinking about statements like, "Science is too complicated to understand." I disagree with that. That's built up by scientists to create a barrier for entry: "This is my tower; I'm building it up so you layman don't get in." I thoroughly disagree. Scientists need to describe phenomena in a language that laymen can understand. Very few do that.

Glen

So scientific jargon is a way to keep scientists in their ivory tower?

Chin

Yes. "We're a special breed. You guys don't understand it. Just listen to us."

Glen

Thinking out loud here. Wasn't Trump's election a rebellion against that?

Chin

That's right. You see it on the financial side, too. I took ECON 101. It's logical: labor and exchange of goods and services. But why is it made so complicated that one needs a specialized post-secondary degree to fully grasp? Ordinary citizens know what they see and experience. They're seeing their living standards going down. They see national debts piling sky high.

Glen

And then they blame those who made things so complex, like those who made complex derivatives and mortgage-backed securities. Things were not explained clearly. This resulted in outrage.

Chin

Do they have a point? That's my question.

Glen

I think you're making an interesting point right now.

I have a premise that I think about when teaching: Connect the course to the world. Is that possible, Dr. Chu? Is this a stupid idea?

Chin

The idea of establishing relevance is to me the most effective teaching tool. We have to deliver a certain amount of content that's specified by the state standards and tests. But I think if we teach it properly, that shouldn't take 100% of instructional time. We should be able to cut it significantly and then with the time left establish relevance.

Glen

Could it be something like runoff from pesticides? Any topic?

Chin

Yeah. Oh, yeah. Oh, yeah. Microplastics in the ocean. Because I worry about mercury, forever chemicals. But how to have a proper discussion would be challenging for teachers.

Glen

That's the question. How would you do that in chemistry? Chemistry is really right in line with those questions — microplastics, mercury, right?

Chin

Well, we first need some basic chemistry. And it's a bit taxing but it's necessary background knowledge to grasp what the issue is. But one thing I have found over the years is trying to teach chemistry content through the historical perspective, by telling stories. We can begin to understand science by appreciating the story behind the discovery. My point is a lot of the discoveries happened by serendipity, by persistence in asking the questions, experimentation, and analyzing results. It's such a human drive, curiosity. Humans want to know why things happen. And this is where asking questions is crucial. You need to give students a space to ask any question. That's how human brains organize information. "Why" helps us make neural connections. And it makes the study of science more engaging.

Here's a great example of storytelling. Most people learned in middle school or even earlier that all physical matter is composed of atoms.

The original meaning of *atom* is "uncuttable." So back in the days of Democritus, more than 2,000 years ago, he hypothesized atomism, physical matter composed of tiny, constantly moving invisible particles. He was shockingly close to our current understanding.

Later on, those small particles would be called atoms. But what happened? Democritus got challenged by Aristotle, the big celebrity of his day. Aristotle supported the four-element model: earth, fire, water, air. Then he threw in a fifth element to pacify the religious groups. And his idea became the dogma for the next 1,500 years.

So the question becomes what happened to that 1,500-year detour in our understanding?

The point is, what we know is often understood by what is commonly accepted to be true, by a popular view, which can become authoritative over time. This kind of thinking is pre-scientific. When we don't have a space to debate divergent views and critically analyze the data, we're not doing science.

Also, the scientific method represents a new way of knowing about the physical world compared to the past 10,000 years. This method allows us to try to separate our emotions, biases, and flawed perceptions of the moment. The scientific method relies on analyzing observable results, which requires in-depth conversation about what was observed. If those results are reproducible, then we can begin to create models to help predict the outcome in future experiments.

But if we are hysterical in our language, we're not going to do science well.

Lauren DelPiano

Glen
How do you teach in our chaotic new normal? Where do you see the problems? Part of surviving in it is not to get overwhelmed. It's not getting too stressed in an already stressful job. That's the other thing. Ironically, being conscientious could be a recipe for burnout.

Lauren
And bitterness of just being there.

Glen
Can I just tell you that I think many of us have lost our sense of humor. What a sense of humor does is allow us to talk about things with a sense of humility. At the heart of today's chaotic new normal is the absence of trust, the walking on eggshells, the paranoia of saying something wrong. Having a sense of humor gives people the space to speak imperfectly and yet be heard. How does that play out for you? Take this as you want, in the school, in your life, in the classroom, and in what you teach. Because I think that trust is the crucial thing. Maybe having a sense of humor is an indication of trust?

Lauren
I mean, it's like the bedrock of everything. Yet you can't force people to do anything either. You can't force people to trust. Quite the opposite. And where is that ground? I don't know. My philosophy has always been you have to give people mentors. That was a big moment for me. The

world slowed down during COVID-19 and I tried something new with a mentor.

Say, for example, that you've been teaching metaphor to 10th graders three years in a row in *The Great Gatsby*. You may not have ever really thought about it beyond the one assignment that you keep handing out. But now here you are. You have an open conversation about it with a mentor and start to see things differently. It comes back to trust and that could start with mentors. And so, without that trust, teaching is going to be a long slog. Maybe part of it is that teachers may not trust themselves.

Glen
You think so?

Lauren
Yes, many may be concerned that someone is going to say something that they see as a problem, that they know deep down has been there. And it could be interpreted as a flaw in their personality, fearing that they'll get called out on the carpet.

Glen
Could you give me an example of where that's the case? So you think that teachers may have a predisposition that could foreclose conversations that would allow them to look at things differently?

Lauren
Absolutely. Over the summer I taught this kid. She was failing. Struggled to do the basics. It was a huge transition

for her, from a therapeutic high school to college. Wouldn't turn stuff in.

So I said, "Please do the assignments. I'm giving you an opportunity to succeed. You have a lot of good things going for you. Make peace with you. We all struggle in different ways. Let's figure out how to move forward." The point for me is that I didn't take it personally when that student didn't hand things in. If I didn't trust myself as a teacher, I would have foreclosed myself from several important conversations with the student.

Glen
Yeah, but why is being at peace with who you are an important part of trust?

Lauren
Because I think otherwise people will take everything personally all the time.

Glen
So here's a question. So you and I share an understanding that to learn stuff you have to be afforded a space in which to make mistakes. Get good feedback. Try again. And on a good day, students will help give their peers meaningful feedback so that there's a sense of teamwork. That's on a really good day. But regardless, I think part of the problem is that there is a certain fragility that students (maybe we all) have. There's this drama: "Oh, I have to redo this? This isn't good enough?" And then there's this feeling of self-doubt at the thought of mistakes. There's

anxiety. Has that transpired in your class? How have you tried to navigate through it?

Lauren

A lot of what I teach is by students learning at their own pace. It completely changed our dynamic. And that was really one of the main reasons why I wanted to change since COVID-19, because kids would tell me they were afraid of me, that I wasn't approachable.

Glen

Wait. You're saying that you changed? Can you "A - B" that?

Lauren

Before, if you didn't turn assignments in on time, I was like, "I'm really sorry. It was due at the end of class. Tough luck. You know I can't accept it because, if I accept it from you, well, I've got to take it from everyone who decided to leave it in their folder or not do it at all."

I just had so many painful conversations with students. It was so simple: "These are the rules. I operate by the rules," and so misguided. But no one wants to live in that world. Let's be real. No one wants to live there. I didn't want to live there. But they were the rules. And it was misguided: It's my way or the highway.

Also, if you did poorly on a test, I didn't really have a gauge on whether a kid cared about my class, whether a kid tried. Ever. Whether they ever made progress, no gauge whatsoever. Prior to changing over to a more growth-based model, I couldn't appreciate their progress. I could maybe look at their grades. But none of it ever seemed connected in a way that was meaningful. None of it ever seemed totally valid. How does taking a test on this day prove that you really understand this skill or content? Maybe you just really like that book. Maybe you read SparkNotes. I don't know. There was no indicator.

I just had no control over my craft. So then I switched. Mainly because I couldn't go on doing what I was doing. It just didn't make any sense.

Glen
And then you switched.

Lauren
I had signed up for this workshop with a mentor. It was $1,000 for me to do it. It was very intense, like you had to submit an application. It was a college class. You had to submit assignments. I had to call this lady and get feedback. But it was fun. I could tell that I was doing it completely differently from others. And she was really receptive and said, "I never thought about doing it this way." And she gave me great feedback. It was working, because previously I didn't know where students were.

Glen
Could you describe what it is like? What's the change?

Lauren
So now I value progress and grit; that's what I'm asking for in a real way. Show me that you're putting in the time

and you're actually growing, because it's very hard in a writing class, despite AI, to fake that. It really is.

Glen

And so now what? What's happened now that you've gone from grades to growth?

Lauren

Well, it changes every single conversation. Every conversation I have with parents is completely different.

Glen

From what to what?

Lauren

Well, it was just sort of combative. Right off the bat, there was a problem: "You're going to fix this problem. Tell me what you're going to do to fix it, Mrs. DelPiano."

And I agree: "There is a problem. Johnny didn't do anything all week. That's why there's a zero in the grade book. What's Johnny doing?"

Now I can say, "Here's what I can see he's done. There are opportunities for him to turn this thing around. Let's figure this out." And then the entire conversation becomes, "Oh, so you're not trying to screw my kid over. This really is about my kid learning something."

A lot of kids, especially with football, really struggled with time management, because football takes up a lot of time. A lot of these parents were doing the lessons with them.

And I heard from parents, "This was really engaging!" We had great conversations.

Glen
Cool!

Lauren
I really appreciated that. It was nice not to need a defense. Now I feel like I can really just do my job.

Glen
If I can take this a step further. People are stressed out, yet you create a system perhaps to reduce it, like, "It's not about whether you got the A or didn't. It's about can you grow?" which defuses the tension. Does that sound right?

Lauren
I think so. I don't have a lot of conversations that are like, why don't I have an A? It's like "Hustle if you want that A; and hustle if you want a B. Are you showing progress?"

I just had a conversation with a student who was here after school. She said, "How do I get the points?" I said, "Well, I don't think you really understood the reading." So you're down here [Lauren's pointing to the floor]. I know you're struggling to understand the reading. Let's deal with that first, because you can't meet the expectation if you don't get the reading. Once we get there, we can get to next steps. Let's honor what you don't know. When you're ready for the next steps, we'll have a conversation, Thursday, if you're ready."

Now this student might not be ready until the end of the year, and what's really nice is, I think people respond to that. I really do. Even the toughest parent tends to respond to that. Where is your kid starting from? We can work from their starting point to help students grow.

Glen
Respond to what?

Lauren
I had a student who was in resource in 8th grade and was bumped up to ICS in 9th grade. Nothing irked me more. I thought, this kid's really going to struggle big time, because I know what the rigor is like. I don't know if this kid's ever written an essay. He started at the bottom. And you could imagine asking him to retry things over and over again when he barely understood any assignment. It was extremely frustrating for him. So what does he do? He goes home and he tells his mother it's too hard. She doesn't know the whole story, that he can retry as many times as he wants, etc. So we have this conversation, and you know, ultimately, all the classic themes come up. Was I too hard? Is he getting enough extra help? Are you doing a good job?

And it all comes to a halt when I say, "Where is he starting from?" OK, he's starting from down here. And what were you expecting? Not of me. What are you expecting of him? Is it for him to be all the way up here? What are you doing to your child? Now I'm going to give him all the opportunities and then I'm going to work with my ICS teacher to make sure that he has all the chances he needs to do well. But a lot of this starts with the fact that they took him out of where he was likely properly placed. Maybe I'm wrong. I'm not a special ed teacher. But you have to be fair to your child and have a sense of what skills they bring to the classroom.

Then the conversation became productive. I told her you can watch every one of my lessons and let me know if there's something you like to change. And in fact, she did it. It was helpful for her. But instead of it becoming a question of am I being fair, it became a matter of helping students grow from where they are.

Glen
Great. Can you comment with regard to the mental state of students?

Lauren
I think so. I mean at the end of summer class, we had a big fishbowl conversation. Alright, so my college freshmen were doing a reflection through their journey and growth as writers. It was a topic of conversation, and a lot of them came back to the fact that high school didn't prepare them for college.

Glen
This is what the college students said? Yes, right?

Lauren
And these are kids who are coming from completely different walks of life. I mean, this one girl was obviously

affluent from a very, very conservative community. Then I've got kids who are in resource rooms or therapy schools who never wrote an essay in their life and yet are taking a college English class at an accelerated pace in the summer. I mean …

Glen
Could be tough.

Lauren
And then there were freshmen who kind of floated through. Not a single student felt they were prepared for college. Every single one of them. Yet they were stuck to their phones but resented any efforts to get them to leave their phones in their dorms. They resented every single effort by administrators to reduce their cell phone usage while fully acknowledging that it damaged their mental health and interrupted their focus.

One of the big takeaways really scared me. I overheard some students having a conversation. And what were they talking about? College made them think critically but they didn't even realize that that's what they were talking about. They described it as thinking about one thing for a long time, writing an essay about something, then having a conversation with somebody about it; and then going back to the essay and teaching yourself more on what you were writing. They claimed that they had never had that experience before. I don't know if I believe them. I think some of these students were incredibly lonely, who claimed to be media savvy and connected. But to me it seemed like they never experienced a moment of silence. They were always plugged in and yet alone. It goes back to this idea that I've been ruminating on: Once we forget things in history, then they're truly forgotten. What a horrible thought. You never get back what's forgotten. Like these ancient things that we've lost.

Glen
Or your grandparents and great-grandparents' wisdom or stories.

Lauren
Right. And then it's just gone and it's terrible. It's terrible.

Glen
It's gone.

Lauren
It's like one of the worst things.

Glen
A terrible silence.

Lauren
Yeah, and I feel like a lot of my students live there, not knowing what they don't know but should: knowing themselves, knowing how to engage in conversation, knowing how to read and write without distraction.

I was talking to a teacher the other day, and we were talking about how so many kids in middle school aren't aware of their accommodations. On a philosophical level,

I think there's something really problematic there. I mean, we're not talking about a kindergartener. I'm talking about a 12-year-old who's struggling with coping with being on the spectrum. They need to know that this is something you need to work on: "Look at how you behaved in this situation? It's not OK and this is happening a lot. Here's how to deal with this."

If this student is not aware that they are on the spectrum, this conversation can take on a negative, even stigmatizing dimension. Having autism is not a character flaw. Having autism does not mean that a student cannot grow or improve by using their strengths. But it starts with self-awareness, with helping students step out of the silence.

Glen

So what you're saying, I think, is that the IEPs are written for the teachers to better accommodate the student, not for the student to better know themselves. I have a story about that. I failed first grade because of bad handwriting, and probably a host of other things like ADHD, etc. So this brought me to a psychologist who gave me a series of tests. And what I remember from these tests at a very early age is that I had above average verbal intelligence and pretty good visual and spatial reasoning. And so, no matter at first grade, no matter what happened afterward — and a lot happened from first through eighth grades — I failed the whole way through. Even though I was lost in a system, I knew I had something. So when I finally got a computer in the ninth grade, I was like, "It's my time. Now I can finally use what I've always known I had."

Lauren
That's really cool. I talk about knowing yourself, because it was so challenging for me as a kid, a kind of trauma that set me back. Had I known myself better in first grade, my life as a student would have been far different. I mean, I don't think I was good at anything in the first grade. I lost most of my kindergarten years because I was sick. I had to get surgery. So I missed a lot. The pediatrician's solution was to keep me out of school. It was weird. And so, I didn't understand why I wasn't doing well in school. Like no one talked to me about it.

Years later, I'm talking with my mom about my own kids, and pushing to get them accommodations, which has been a process. It's so different now.

As I'm going through the process to create accommodations for my son, my mom said, "Well, they wanted to classify you."

And I said, "Really, that's fascinating. Why didn't you do it? Because elementary school was hell for me on every front, because I had lost so much time." (Thank God I grew up on a block full of kids. Otherwise, I would have had no friends. Like no social skills. It would have been horrible!)

And she said, "We didn't want to stigmatize you!"

So, I thought, "Don't want to let them do what? Help me?"

Because the fact of the matter is, I went through eight grades thinking I was a complete idiot. I didn't know what was wrong with me. My neighbor across the street was getting As like she knew everything. And I'm crying on the way home because I knew my state tests would come back bad.

And my parents would not look kindly on that, while my neighbor would do really well. And her mother would say, 'Well, I'm sure you tried your best.'"

And I'm like "You don't understand. I don't even know what my best is! I have no idea what's going on, you know?"

And I feel like a lot of students live in that silence in a place of personal ignorance. And it's just so terrible. It's like, let's just talk about you. What is going on? What are you struggling with? What don't you know? What don't you get about this question? It's not a plague. We'll figure it out. Being able to have that conversation has been such a game changer for me. But even more than that, students need feedback. They need to be heard.

Ellen Hill

Glen
How do you teach in our chaotic new normal?

Ellen
I know that your hypothesis is that today's problems are different. And I think for our students it is different. To be honest, I think they are feeling it is. They are internalizing it.

Glen
Why do you say that?

Ellen
I've been teaching twenty-eight years here, thirty-three years overall. I taught in New York City for two years in Bed-Stuy and overseas for three years before that.

Climate change and its impact on society, these kids now understand that. They see the results they're living in. There are massive superstorms and hurricanes and mudslides. You can't get away from it. You know, Greta Thunberg, and that whole movement? Many of my students are invested in what she's saying. She's educating them. And young people are disappointed in us. So that is different. The kids are much more aware now than they were twenty-eight years ago.

Glen
So, there's a sense of doom?

Ellen
Yes, absolutely. And hopelessness, absolutely. They feel like it's out of their control and that the adults in the room aren't listening; and by the time they'll become adults, it will be too late. That's how they're feeling, and they are majorly depressed. They are. They're bipolar, they're clinically depressed, they are — it's an epidemic. The mental health crisis is real. This is not just something that's making headlines. I think these students want to raise awareness. That's what they want to do. Because eventually they're going to be the adults in the room.

Glen
And this is what the science is ... I was reading about it ... global warming is imminent. Like if we don't change course, like, now ... global warming is going to go past three to four degrees and we're cooked...

Ellen
Right. I agree with you. How is this, high school, relevant when the world is on fire? When the world is on fire, why is doing homework important, right? Many feel like there is no purpose to some of them living. They're not just depressed. They just don't want to be here.

Glen
On planet Earth?

Ellen

Right. Many of them don't want to ever have children. They speak of this freely. They don't want to have children because why would you want to have another human life in this world? This is not a handful of students. This is something that they talk about a lot.

Glen
How do you know this?

Ellen
We don't specifically talk about eco-anxiety, but while they're doing their work, there's freedom. They're doing labs, they're doing group activities, they finish at different points, in different groups, and they bring these things up on their own. I'm not pointedly eliciting the information in these discussions. I think that's what's different, how this chaotic new normal is affecting them.

I keep my personal opinions personal. Right back when I first started teaching, it was all about bioethical issues. Remember Dolly, the cloned sheep? That's when I started working here. It was the cloned sheep, and it was about using pig parts in humans or cow parts in humans.

So that leads to a whole set of issues. I knew at the time how I felt about those things. But I have to teach them from the factual, scientific standpoint and let the students make their own decisions on how they feel about them morally.

Glen
And now?

Ellen

And now I do the same thing. I mean, I always have. But climate change, unfortunately, has become a political issue. Maybe not as much today as eight years ago? I like to think that we've come further along in the conversation in the last eight years, when during presidential debates people on the debate stage said they didn't "believe in global warming." I don't think we're still there, are we?

Glen

I don't know, but I think it trails with the election denial, which is about one-fourth to one-third of the population.

Ellen

One-third of the population? That's embarrassing.

So I have been teaching ecology. It's a major unit. It's one of the four major topics in biology at the high school level, right? There's molecular biology, genetics, evolution, and ecology. Therefore, I've been teaching ecology forever. We talk about the carbon cycle and how the carbon dioxide in the atmosphere has increased due to human interference, how that plays out with climate and weather patterns.

I've taught and said for the last thirty-three years, climate change isn't something you believe in or don't believe in. If you say that you sound ignorant. Climate change is a fact, and I can show you how the climate is changing. When I look at different amounts of carbon dioxide in the atmosphere or methane over time, I can look at the temperature. Those are measurable. That's science; that's facts. So please don't say that you believe or don't believe in climate change or global warming. You need to understand that how we deal with these facts is what's debatable. Not that they are facts, but how do we go forward. How do we balance this with the economy?

Glen

That's interesting, because we have this really urgent problem. And then all of a sudden you have a couple smart-sounding people who could say, "I'm not so sure," like the Malone guy who claims to be an expert in virology. *The New York Times*[16] writes that he spreads false news. Still, a consensus gets squashed in the United States. Not everyone is for the vaccine. Then conspiracy theorists glom onto it. Algorithms are attracted to that outrage and spread it.

Ellen

It's my job as a science teacher to teach my students how to look at that information. Who it's coming from and analyze it. If one person says it, but ninety-nine people say the opposite, shouldn't students be able to think critically and figure out where the truth is? You know, are you saying that this man who's the outlier has any evidence?

Glen

---

[16] Alba, D. (2022, April 3). *The latest covid misinformation star says he invented the vaccines.* The New York Times. https://www.nytimes.com/2022/04/03/technology/robert-malone-covid.html

No. I don't even know what he's talking about. I just know that Joe Rogan just had him on, and he went viral. The New York Times says he spreads falsehoods about vaccines.[17] Then conspiracy theorists about the vaccine echoed his points. I have family members who buy into it. That's part of the problem.

So another example, the election. I know teachers are scared to say anything regarding the election, and yet it's an essential conversation for the health of our democracy.

Ellen

I don't say anything about whom to vote for, but I definitely encourage all of my students to register to vote. And to be informed. I think that's one of my jobs, to create an informed electorate. You know, different science teachers have different emphases, and mine has always been, since I started here, that students should be able to analyze where they get their news. That's always been my angle. And I never let them know what my position is. And if they assume it, I always play devil's advocate.

Here's what I mean by critical thinking: We start AP Biology with an ecology unit because we don't often get the time to develop that in Honors Biology. It's one of the

---

[17] Alba, D. (2022, April 3). The latest covid misinformation star says he invented the vaccines. New York Times. Retrieved from https://www.nytimes.com/2022/04/03/technology/robert-malone-covid.html.

eight units in AP, a very descriptive topic that's usually their summer assignment.

They have to make believe that they are on a marketing team that was hired to get people to vote a certain way on an issue, like should we drill in the Arctic or not? Should we limit the amount of carbon coming out of a car?

And they have to convince a voter to vote yes or no. They make believe it is a question on a ballot, a referendum. I had to show them examples of public questions on a ballot where you either vote yes or no.

They create a brochure that would be mailed to a voter's house. It had to say "Vote yes because ..." And they not only had to support why someone should vote yes, but why the other side was wrong. They had to refute the other side's opinion.

It was so hard for them to do that. I just don't think they were used to doing it. They're used to "my way or the highway."

Glen
So do younger teachers feel the same way, or do you think that there's a fear to discuss issues? You have issues of science that are on the ballot. Perhaps the political aspects make teachers scared to address them? Is that part of the problem?

Ellen

I think it depends on the individual, how confident that person is. There are younger teachers in this district who absolutely have no problem bringing up controversial issues, and there are others who probably do shy away from it. It's up to the individual. I think it also depends on what district you teach in.

We are sitting here in a school that is in upper-middle class, in a mid-Atlantic state, in New Jersey, in one of the best counties for education in the country, statistically, with a board of education that's supportive.

I live two towns away. Completely different story. And this is what you're referring to, because their board of education has become so political, in my town, which potentially could happen anywhere in any town. You may have read it in the paper. I watch the board meetings virtually. I have a lot going on in my life right now, so it's just not a priority to follow it very closely.

But there are other people taking up the fight. And guess who it is? It's the students who are speaking out against book bans. The issue happened to come up from people who ran for the board of ed six or seven years ago. They almost won. Two years later, they did.

They ran on banning books that talked about teen suicide. Actually, *13 Reasons Why*. Meanwhile, there's a Netflix series and parents really, in my opinion, should have been sitting down with their child if their child was interested in this.

131

Sit down and watch the Netflix series with your kid. First, read the book and talk about it with your child. Right? Not talking about suicide isn't going to prevent it. Any mental health professional will tell you the best thing to do is actually to talk about it, if you're going to prevent it.

But people ran on the platform of banning this book. (Meanwhile, students could go to any public library and get it out. They could watch it on Netflix. It's at the point of absurdity.) They were not in the majority until last year. So now policies are being written from this perspective. And students are not happy.

They banned the pride flag a year ago. And what they did [the school administration] was state that only the American flag and the New Jersey flag could be flown on school property. OK, that's how they worded it so it didn't sound discriminatory.

As a result, the students put up pride flag lawn signs.

Well, students were told, that's a picture of a flag and it has to be removed.

Students insisted the school was just discriminating against this population and this idea.

Now students created signs that had rainbow-colored bubbles on them that read "[Insert Town Name] has Pride."

Well, guess what? Those were removed.

The temporary superintendent resigned over this. He couldn't take it. So now this. They had a very contentious board meeting in April of just this past year. This is all in the *Bergen Record.* It's embarrassing.

The students actually stood up and said you can take away all the signs you want. We're still here. We're not going anywhere.

Glen
You know what I realize while talking to you is that science, as contentious as the topics may be, is undergirded by data, whereas other subjects are not. For example, issues related to sexuality and gender — whatever social and biological issues — there's this perception of gray areas, kind of how global warming or vaccine hesitancy is argued from various sources.

Just to give you an example of this, which partly inspired this book, is that one of my students was at the Stop the Steal Rally on January 6, 2021. He was on the capitol steps. Now I know him well. I've had dinner with him, had hikes with him. We've had numerous conversations for hours. And I ask him, "What were you thinking? Where are your facts? What are you talking about?"

Ellen
And he stands by that, by what he did?

Glen
Yes. But the point is, you have data on your side, double-blind placebos, a rigorous standard set by a cohort of

scientists. Students of social studies or language arts lack that kind of rigor across the board. It becomes much more interpretive, much more of a jury of your peers.

Yet it was impossible for us, no matter our hikes, etc., to have that kind of discovery, as if during a court case, where we could agree on the facts. But to get to that place of agreeing on the facts at times seems Herculean. That's the problem. But maybe it's different in teaching science?

Ellen
That's a great question.

Glen
Right. Right. You're not promoting your political agenda. You're helping them discover the facts.

Ellen
A couple years ago, some students were very vocal about their opinions. They happened to be conservative — doesn't matter to me. They were in a senior class of mine and had a big chip on their shoulder about how their teachers were so liberal.

They were talking about a particular teacher that they had who's no longer here, how he kept asking them to defend their position. And they thought that approach — defend your position — made him so liberal.

And I said, "Maybe he's just trying to make you think. Maybe he's playing devil's advocate. Did you guys ever think that was a learning experiment to get you to think and back up your views with facts?"

And they're like, "Oh, we didn't think of that."

Now, whether or not that was this teacher's goal, I have no idea. I wasn't there, but it made them think about it, at least in a different way.

Now a topic that's a biggie is evolution, right? And I've even had parents talk to me about this twice in my twenty-eight years.

I used to survey students about this for perhaps my first ten years here. They were mostly freshmen, so let's keep that in mind. Not juniors and seniors that I teach now. And I asked them about creationism and evolution.

Every year it was consistent. A third of the students reported believing in creationism. I think that's a very high number. A third, 33%. And it didn't deviate very much every year that I did it.

I used to talk to them about how creationism is part of your faith. You learned it in your faith, right? And faith, by definition, is believing without seeing what you have faith in. And science is really the opposite. In science, we don't believe without observing facts under experimental conditions where repeated results help form a conclusion.

We talked about the difference between those two. I asked my students to go to their elders and talk to them about faith — their parents, their grandparents — and see what they think. Ask them.

Glen

Yeah, it's a great point because if creationism is part of your worldview, I would suspect, embrace the faith. You don't want to conflate your cherished beliefs with science because, why would you put your faith against the strictest of scientific scrutiny to invalidate your faith? Seems like two different approaches that are best kept separate, right?

Ellen

So that's why I said, you know, I've been dealing with these controversial bioethical issues in the ecology units, in evolution, and in the genetics units for a long time.

Glen

So how do you talk about issues such as AI or microplastics? Don't these kinds of issues contribute to mental health problems?

Ellen

I try to tell the students who come to me in confidence that there are certain things they can control. Let's start small. How can you make a difference? How can you make a difference in your family? I mean simple little things, right? Use reusable bottles instead of one-use plastic bottles. If you have to fight with your parents about it, fight with them. Show them why this is better. You control what you can.

Glen

When you're talking to 100 students a year, you could have a huge network effect. Say, 50% of those kids spread that message.

Ellen
You have control over that.

Glen
The thing that you just said really interests me.

Ellen
That's because you posed that question about teaching today. I don't think my teaching has changed, because in every one of the major units I teach, there have been controversial issues throughout time. But what has changed is my students because of what those issues mean to them.

Glen
I understand. How does this impact you? How do you process these big problems within yourself?

Ellen
It's a responsibility! Teach citizenship! We all have to teach that. They should be informed. It's my job to teach them how to be informed, not indoctrinate.

GLEN COLEMAN

Anonymous

Glen
So what comes to mind when you hear "How to teach in our chaotic new normal?"

Anonymous
My first thoughts are all the expectations.

I feel like teaching has evolved so much. Twenty percent of what we do is teaching and the rest is about fulfilling other expectations. Like one of the biggest things is differentiation. Reaching every single learner, yes, that's part of teaching. But differentiation feels like a setup for failure. Is it realistic that I could lesson-plan, teach, and grade for seventy students? Even if I leveled it, how do I reach everyone in a way that satisfies a bureaucracy that's not in the classroom?

I have, say, five levels of learners in a class: the very, very low students with a reading level of second grade; then the next level slightly below grade level; then the average; then I have the kids who need enrichment; and then beyond. And again, I don't know how it's structured where you live, but here, we have students who might be pulled out for their reading and math.

Then I'm supposed to teach life skills. But I teach history. So expectations right off the bat is where I'm hitting my biggest frustration. How am I supposed to do all that, every lesson, every day, all the time? It takes up my time

138

and energy. Then I'm to prepare lessons and teach as well?

Glen
In your school, are they putting a hammer to you guys?

Anonymous
Not so much, but I feel just the societal expectation of what I'm supposed to be doing for every single kid. All of these competing expectations are a root problem for me.

Another example beyond differentiation is social emotional learning. I get the idea of teaching, for example, mindfulness, but I teach social studies. Am I now a guidance counselor? It's another layer and then another layer. And I understand how it can be incorporated, but it's one more thing that I'm now planning for, looking at how these students are going to practice social emotional learning while working in small groups. It's just one more thing to document, another random thing that comes up daily. Like we have active shooter drills. I just had training on how to pack a bullet wound. I'm not saying that some of the training isn't valid. Maybe I should know how to pack a bullet wound in case that happens. But then I'm to learn how to pile the desks in my classroom against a shooter and how to differentiate instruction and social emotional learning? All these different roles ... I feel like what I'm now taking on is just so much.

Glen
You spoke about packing a bullet wound. That's astonishing. And then you spoke about these competing

expectations, which is a great topic, too. So how does this show up for you in your day-to-day? Are there experiences you could recount where maybe the administration is putting that over your head — or maybe parents — so that in the back of your mind, you say to yourself, "*H*ow am I going to balance all of this?"

Anonymous
Well, I don't know if it necessarily relates completely, but I was sitting in an IEP meeting. Some students need accommodations to learn. And one of the accommodations was that they wanted the student to have no homework. Not that he *can't* do the homework. They don't want him to have homework because of a sport that this child is in. And so that was actually shot down. Rightfully so by the IEP team as a whole, specifically because of the special education teacher.

But the parent then said, well, then he's just not gonna do it anyway and take the 0. Then they were trying to insinuate that we weren't meeting the needs of their child. It wasn't computing for me that we're not meeting the needs of the child because we're not doing exactly what the parents said.

And so I think that is a big problem, too. Parents now expect this customer service relationship rather than doing what's in the best interest of the child educationally. Parents want to hear the word "Yes." "Yes, I will do whatever you say," neglecting that we are the professionals looking out for the best interests of the child, that education is not like going to McDonald's. It's about helping children become responsible adults and critical thinkers. The customer service model does not help to that end. Often parents seem to be saying to the student, "Yes, you're right. We'll do everything you want no matter what," even things that are outrageous. I had a parent once in a meeting for accommodations say that every single time this child wasn't paying attention, that I re-review and repeat the entire lesson again. I'm like, "How am I supposed to ... what do the other kids do?" But the parents had the expectation that whatever they want, they get, no matter what it is.

I don't know if that ties so closely, but ...

Glen

I think it does. I think people have been getting increasingly anxious for a number of reasons. First is that technology is getting smarter than we are and threatening jobs. So we have to keep our skills sharp. Otherwise, who's going to prepare the kids for the future? The second thing is that technology is working overtime on our brain. It's giving us cotton candy. So we're getting this diet of crap, which is resulting in depression and anxiety all around.

Anonymous
Right.

Glen

And last, students are supposed to learn about the world, but it's in rough shape right now. It's creating this cauldron of upset. Maybe that's leading some overwhelmed parents to exclaim, "Don't brainwash our kids!"

Anonymous
Right.

Glen
And then it goes viral. The algorithm loves the outrage.

Anonymous
Exactly. Exactly. Yes. I feel like that's definitely part of it, too. I feel like everything that I say or do could potentially be taken and criticized and completely turned against me.

Glen
Could you relay a story or even just a moment in which you thought, "Oh my goodness, this could be really bad."

Anonymous
Yeah, this is not even from teaching. This actually just happened from coaching. I coach bowling and I'm a very sarcastic person all the time, and my students know that. We were working on technique, and some of them couldn't get it. And unbeknownst to me, they were filming me, because apparently, they all think that they're TikTokers and vloggers. They film everything. But one bowler couldn't quite get it. He was new to the game. I said something off-the-wall like, "This is a whole new level of bad." It made him giggle and feel better. But then

I found out that some other bowlers were recording the conversation. And they were going to post it. I literally thought about this for 36 hours nonstop, because all it would take is for them to post that and then ... boom. Front page in the news: coach tells their player, "You suck." You see front page headlines of teachers all the time. Anything said innocently or playfully could just totally be turned around and ruin your career.

Glen
That's horrifying and so relevant.

Anonymous
Apparently, vlogging is a big thing in our school, recording classes, then cutting videos together, and posting online. Like, "Here's my day." And I think, all they have to do is cut the wrong piece out of context, and that's it. It's over. Everything is over. Yeah, it's scary.

Glen
...one more piece of stress. I remember ... I don't know if you were teaching at this point, but I remember when I was teaching during the invasion of Afghanistan after 9/11. In our classroom, we had really good conversations. I still remember the kids. Still see their faces. I never thought that I was being recorded. But I don't think today's conversations are as good. I think people are scared. Students might not even know it. It's like the fear has become normalized.

Anonymous

Right, definitely. I mean, social media has taken the element of conversation away. But then we're supposed to be teaching through conversation.

Glen
Could you expound on that? Why do you think that is happening? Like how do you see that?

Anonymous
That social media has taken away the art of conversation? At this point, social media is their lives and how they live their lives, at least for many students. Also, students are judged through social media. They've learned that if they put "this" out there and it's different from what somebody else thinks, they're going to be judged for it. So they're just not going to share and yet they're not going to be liked for not sharing. And I think that feeds into the classroom, too.

Glen
I'm going to throw out a couple of things. January 6. COVID-19. Did those things contribute to the craziness?

Anonymous
Yes and no. I mean, I personally wouldn't touch the political stuff with a 10-foot pole.

Glen
Why not?

Anonymous

Oh, absolutely not, because I say one thing, or I encourage any type of discussion that one side doesn't like, and I'm getting a phone call for sure.

Glen
How do you know?

Anonymous
Let me tell you this story. This didn't happen to me personally. A colleague of mine had a flag that was torn. He took it down to have it replaced. The next day he gets a phone message that says he must hate America. He's clearly against America because he's not flying his flag. The very next day.

Things are politically charged. The second you bring something up, anything can be misinterpreted. So you open yourself up to scrutiny when you address controversial topics. So why do it? It's not worth it. As much as that could create good conversation, it's not worth it. I would much rather take a safe route and keep my job for the next however many years rather than risk it.

Glen
I'm playing devil's advocate because I'm wrestling with this question. It's the kind of thing that keeps me up at night. What if people have become so politicized that students can't talk to each other? So this whole thing that I created for myself — connect the classroom to the world — has become much more difficult. So what is it like

where you teach? Does the environment there contribute to the problem?

Anonymous
It's very divided, and I think that's the problem. We have hardcore Republicans and hardcore Democrats. It's extremely divisive. And I hear kids come in and say things that they don't even know what they're saying. They're clearly repeating things that their parents said. And it would be great to then dig in and use that to teach them how to actually look up things, platforms, politicians, and policies. But no. My God, no. Because if I teach them how to do that and then they change their mind and go against their parents, oh God. Forget it. Forget it. It's just not worth it. I need to support my family. I would absolutely get a phone call. And probably wouldn't be allowed to talk about it anyway.

Can I give you an example? This is not political. This is absolutely something that happened. We were doing a lesson on rituals, on which religious ritual is important to you, because we have a diverse group of students and we wanted to represent all cultures and have people have a chance to share their experiences. We had them make presentations. Kids were so excited about this lesson. Then we got a phone call from a parent. One student didn't want to participate. OK, that's absolutely fine. We said we could come up with an alternative. No problem. But that wasn't good enough. The parent said, "We don't want anyone doing the project, because if my child can't do it then it's not fair. No one can do it." And wouldn't you know the entire assignment was canceled for every student. So why would I do something political where it's going to take one phone call that ends the assignment for everybody. It's just not worth it, and the assignment that got canceled wasn't even political or controversial.

The insinuation was that it's not our place to talk about someone's culture. It wasn't about being "woke." It turned into the warped idea that teachers shouldn't even be asking the question. It's really just one person who complains and yells the most. That person is going to get their way. And people are going to complain and yell about anything. It would be such a lost cause even if I didn't get fired or disciplined. It would just be shut down from the start. So why put in the time?

Glen
How did other parents respond? Were they disappointed?

Anonymous
Nobody knew.

Glen
OK, so did the administration just caved?

Anonymous
Yep, definitely. The assignment was over.

Glen
That's a scary story. I mean, if you can't talk about a religion or a religious ritual, like introducing yourself to

GLEN COLEMAN

your classmates, which is basically what you're doing, then how do you talk about other questions? I mean the First Amendment is partly about protecting everyone's voice and protecting everyone's religious freedoms and such.

Any concerns about January 6 or election denial? Especially as a social studies teacher, this is one of the most significant events that we've lived through. If a critical mass thinks the election is illegitimate, how can our democracy survive?

Anonymous
Right.

Glen
How does that affect your view of this whole teaching thing or of the shitstorm we're in?

Anonymous
I mean, honestly, not. I don't think about that a whole lot, only because that's not the component of history that I'm teaching. I teach Colonial America. So we're right before they get to this idea of democracy. I see others staying the hell away from it and not discussing it in class. I don't really think about it.

Glen
I think yours is the rule, not the exception around the United States. Most don't want to (or can't) teach it.

Anonymous

I think everybody knows that's wrong. When you try to do what's right, it always ends up a negative. Back to the story about rituals. We tried to do what was right by highlighting cultures, and then that was "wrong." So, why go beyond that? I need my job. The administration's words say one thing, but their actions say something else.

Also, it's like everyone is saying, we need to teach critical thinking and problem-solving, and whenever I do that, parents, administrators, or the board of education will fire me for doing it. It goes down to the basics of behavioral learning. If I do this, I get a consequence. So I'm not going to do it anymore and not get the consequence. I don't need to be shocked 1,000 times. It doesn't make sense, but if I don't do it, then nobody says anything to me. OK, great. Then that's what I'm gonna do.

Glen

Do you see kids trying to start a conversation in class?

Anonymous

So I teach the topic of American slavery, which is very divisive. We stick to a lot of facts, a lot of primary sources.

You can see kids are even afraid to ask questions because they know that if they say something the wrong way, even with positive intent, it doesn't matter. You say one wrong thing and you're labeled as that kid forever. I see them wanting to maybe ask, but they know. They know the repercussions, so they're not doing it either. And I don't blame them.

I wanted them to read this short story about Harrison Bergeron. We wanted to add it into our curriculum. This was just the meeting that we had today. The story is actually from the 60s, but it's set in like 2083. It's this dystopian future where they take equality to the extreme. Everyone has to be the same amount of good looking. So if you're a really good-looking person, they give you prosthetics and you have to wear them or else you go to jail. If you are very smart, you get a chip put in your head that has this beep that interrupts your thoughts and prevents you from critically thinking — equality taken to the extreme.

We were discussing among colleagues whether people were going to say that we're saying equality is bad? We immediately started by asking what repercussions would come if we read this? Forget the amazing character depth. Forget the themes that could be present. Forget the discussions that will happen. That's our first thought before anything else.

Glen
What's amazing about that is nobody's talking to us about this larger problem that I think we're in. Why isn't the National Council for Social Studies taking a stand? Why isn't some professional organization bringing us together, or teachers from other disciplines, or unions, or concerned citizens? Why hasn't the NCSS sent an email to every single social studies teacher in the country to say, "We need to talk about this."

Anonymous

Right.

Glen

Instead, it's a solo venture, which makes us more scared. It isn't like I can say, "Hey, I'm doing this on behalf of the National Council for Social Studies (or whatever your discipline) or the Constitution and this is what we stand for." It feels like many of us are lost.

So here, here's one of the final questions that comes to mind. I think one of the problems is that we're alone. And it's weird to say, because I don't know exactly what the opposite looks like. I've been teaching for twenty-six years in the same school. It's hard to imagine other possibilities. Do you have a similar experience?

Anonymous

No, I think that's one thing our school is extremely blessed to have. We have not only our prep time, but we have team planning time where all history teachers get together and discuss what we're doing, how we're doing it, when we're doing it, and what changes we want to make. This is something that our union fought for. But I don't know if that's normal. We have common planning time every day. Every day, we get to meet together. And so I do feel very blessed in that regard.

But I'm still in the classroom alone. Don't get me wrong. We still have free creative teaching license, but we certainly have an opportunity to collaborate, like, "Hey, what are you doing? How are you doing it? How did this go for you? What did you think about this?" I do feel really lucky to have that. It makes a huge difference, because I get new ideas. I can see if someone's doing something better than I am and then I get to hear their perspectives, and vice versa. And it's amazing. But I will say we always end up on the same page about these different issues. We still are not bold enough to say, "Yep, let's take that on." We agree to refrain from those adventures.

Glen
Right. So maybe you guys could agree not to discuss potentially explosive topics. So you guys are on the same page?

Anonymous
The same page exactly. So we all know exactly the things that we're staying away from. If I come up with this idea that I'm gung ho about, then they share their horror story of what happened the one time they did do that. I'm like, "Well, better not do that then. Thanks."

Glen
So what is it like for you to be that sole person as a teacher alone in the classroom with your students?

Anonymous
Maybe I'm the only one who does this, who goes back to that internal monologue. I go home and replay everything: do I think that they think "this"? What if I had said "this" differently? Or checking my email ten times because I said that "one thing." Is "it" going to get me a phone call tomorrow? It's just constant. It's constant because there's no one there to validate what's

happening. There's no one there to validate, "You're fine. That was perfectly fine. It's OK." Or there's no one there to even buffer.

Let's say I start to discuss something potentially controversial. For instance, we were talking about the mistreatment of the Native Americans by Columbus and the mass murder that he committed and the topic of rape is difficult to address. But it was common. It's the history. Discussing it accurately reflects the historical record. Could we almost say it without saying it? But there's no one there to help me in the classroom. There's no one to help redirect or recontextualize, knowing full well it's a perfectly valid topic to be discussing and it's accurate ... but maybe it can be addressed better? There's no one there to be a buffer. So most of the time, it's the other way. Things are perfectly fine, but I need some validation to know if I'm hitting the targets I'm aiming for.

Glen

Yeah. And what's fascinating about this — to get a little bit meta — is that democracy is about conversation. It's about tolerance. It's about trying to figure it out together and experimenting. So, what you're describing is a kind of siege. You're surrounded by competing stimuli that you're trying to manage and stave off. You're on the lookout for a preemptive accusation — In other words, blindsided by something you allegedly said that's misrepresented and threatens your job.

Anonymous

Right.

Glen

I just want to say one of my solutions is that every course should be interdisciplinary. Because this way you have two people in the room. Nobody has dominance over the curriculum. And by both teachers creating something new, they learn from each other.

Anonymous
Right.

Glen
Yeah. How does that sound to you? Would that be a good idea?

Anonymous
Oh my gosh, that would completely change school for the better, because the real world is not segmented. The real world isn't history here, math here, and reading here. That's not real life. So why are we doing that, compartmentalizing knowledge?

Saratheresa "ST" Bartelloni

Glen
What does teaching or making art in a chaotic new normal mean to you?

Saratheresa
[We were talking about photography before taping the interview.] So in art, obviously you had the photographer, who was the master of chemistry, the dark room, exposure, light, and aperture. This technical stuff was incredibly specialized. And then came Photoshop. You no longer had to stand there on a foggy day and determine film speed, f-stops, or aperture, and the chemical output of a negative to create a positive in a darkroom. It's been replaced. But there's still value in understanding what goes into making the photograph. When I think about some of the basic tools that I used to teach years ago when I taught photography, we would show them how to do it in the darkroom and then we would show them the counterpart in Photoshop. Then we would explore other tools: the dodging tool, the burning tool. These techniques are trial and error in the dark room and ...

Glen
You can press control-Z in Photoshop.

Saratheresa
You can press control-Z. It's outstanding! When Photoshop first came out, you could only press control-Z once, I think. Now you can control-Z to your heart's

content. But just the other day, I thought of my father, who was a draftsman. He was not an architect, but he would draft plans for a carpenter. So upstairs in his office space, he had a drafting table that was my grandfather's. They hand-drew the plans. You would see the side view, the front view, etc.

My brother is now in construction and does it all digitally. It is amazing how he can now render something immediately from a drawing into three-dimensions. But you still need knowledge and real-world experience of what you're putting into drafting programs.

Glen
But doesn't the computer take more of the work away from the creator? Isn't the computer doing more of the lifting now?

Saratheresa
So just the other day, I found it interesting, because I came up with this doodle. Then I asked one of my art Honor Society kids, who's into graphic design, to come up with an official logo for my new Ukulele Club. In my mind, it was a cartoony hawk, playing a cartoony ukulele, wearing a cartoony lei — festive and fun. I downloaded it and was playing with this idea in Adobe Express, the go-to Photoshop for non-Photoshop users. You can design flyers, websites, brochures, flow charts, like whatever you want. Because we are in an Adobe school, we have access to it. So sure enough, I open it. I was like, "Oh, let

me just play with this." And I noticed that all of a sudden, oh, my God, there's AI, right here!

So I wanted to see what happens. We created a new flyer with an AI image. And then it was like, would you like to see a black and gold hawk playing ukulele? And my mind was blown. Was it what I had pictured in my head, precisely? No. But it was darn close. I was like, wow. That's wild. So it's kind of amazing. Not for nothing, I had to learn computer languages in high school ...

Glen
So wait, you're saying that back then you had to know computer programming, but now it seems as though, per Steve Jobs' dream of programming done by a layperson, you're just putting these conversational commands into the AI, like "black and gold hawk that plays a ukulele," and whammo.

But is this disturbing, too?

Saratheresa
Well, I just gave a demonstration of the pottery wheel to my advanced ceramics students about artificial intelligence. The machinery changes pottery and mass production in general. But the experience of making pottery with clay will never be lost. It's a very mindful activity. There's always going to be a need to create authentic experiences.

Glen
Are you sure about that? What about authentic products?

Saratheresa

And then there will be some things where we don't want an authentic experience. My one daughter really likes to read. She really likes to write. She sometimes fumbles over the writing part, but she loves to read her paragraph out loud. That kind of thing. To a certain extent I think, OK, we got this AI thing. Who's to say that the president's speech writer won't be helped by an AI next year? Future careers and vocations will definitely be changed. I also recognize that content needs to be provided in order for AI to evolve. You need data sets of all sorts: more writing, images, and things like that.

But I think in terms of teaching writing, that will be impressive. It's hard to distinguish. This is not just, "Did you copy somebody's old paper (i.e., let's put it up and turn it in)?" This is intense.

I also know as an AP art teacher, AP currently is saying absolutely in no step of your process can a student use AI. (In the past it used to be the fear of going to Google Images or something that was already out there. Now you could go to AI for art. Type in a concept and see what AI generates that might springboard you into something else.) That is prohibited for AP art. I don't think they're going to be able to stick with that. I think they'll have to evolve, because I can go to a museum and see what an artist has done and allow that to inspire me. Why not for AI? But then does my artwork become part of the data set for AI?

Glen

You know what's amazing about this stuff, Sara, is that you're able to have these thoughts without it messing up your day.

Saratheresa

I'm not going to let this mess up my day, but I will say this. I'm a parent of three, right? So my future is fine. I'm almost there [retirement]. I'm, like, hanging on by a thread. We'll see how much longer I've got. [Chuckle.]

Glen
You got plenty.

Saratheresa

But of course, my youngest is 10, there's a lot of future ahead, hopefully a nice, healthy future. So.
where will AI put him or what will he do with it? My 17-year-old will also have to live in a world with AI.

Glen
Do you not feel any sense of alarm?

Saratheresa

Sometimes it's like I'm in a crazy, ridiculous sci-fi movie. I feel like Will Smith had a movie where the machines were taking over, right? It's like this crazy creature out there, but I'm not going to ... I can't let this ...

Glen

But I don't even hear something willful from you. I don't hear you saying, "I am choosing to think of something else." No, you go about your day as you would any other, enjoying River Dell and your life. But maybe it's easier for you as a creative person in a creative content area.

Saratheresa
Yeah, it's probably a lot easier for me. But I do feel like my job kind of changed when I think of AI. Over the summer I did some research and thought, "Wow! Snap! This is intense. Different." And looking at my own children and thinking, alright, well, my oldest — this isn't in her nature. It isn't like she would say, "Let me search for the answers online." She wants to do the work. She really loves to craft her things. She's not operating in this intense pressure environment that requires perfection, because in my house we don't expect it. But I think about my youngest. AI will have developed substantially. And I wonder what that will mean for him. But in my classroom, I'm looking at it as, this is what they're growing up with, artificial intelligence.

Glen
What do you mean?

Saratheresa
We emerged from a COVID storm. Ramifications are still with us. With my students I'm like, what can I do as one little human on this earth, one little period a day for a total of 120 kids? I try to give them an experience that is so pleasant that somewhere along the line they will crave authenticity. They'll be like, "I actually enjoyed physically doing that. I want to feel that again somewhere." They're

not going to be mosaic artists. On a good day, they're going to make a dish for their grandmother. The idea is for them to tap into some part of their humanity, and make them want to pull that into some other aspect, whether it's working with people or something that they're passionate about.

It's the funniest thing. When you came in and you turned off the radio [in my classroom], I don't even hear it, but when my AP kids came in, they were like, "What's wrong? Something is wrong here today." I was really alarmed and one of my students said, "Miss B. The music's not on." It's not a curated playlist. It's not my personal style of music or their personal style. It is 102.7 FM. It is like five decades of tunes and you never know what they're going to put on. And it has commercials. There's something so freaking simple about it. And it's crazy because kids of all sorts love 102.7 FM on my old clock radio. There's no thinking. There's no consistency. It's unpredictable. There's no Spotify playlist or swipe to the next song. So, it was like you could hear a pin drop. And a student said, "Miss Bartelloni, the tunes aren't on." I was like, "Oh my gosh, how can I forget the tunes?"

Before COVID while we were teaching remotely, I would do Spotify. I would type in a theme, country or jazz. And I would have it playing over my computer as background music because of the microphone on the laptop. There I was, alone in this room. And so I couldn't function just listening to the refrigerator hum. I needed something. So I brought up this box from the basement, thinking,

"Maybe this stupid thing works." The little antenna is stuck on the wall. It's just slung up there so simply and so subtly. And yet it kind of fills a little space. So I appreciate it for its absolute simplicity and what it does to the overall environment. That type of feeling kind of directs me.

But then I came back this school year and I noticed that students were not so nice to each other compared to my earlier years as a teacher. There are specific incidents that come to mind that I will keep private. But those incidents concern me. I wonder why this year, in particular. As I say to my students, "Kindness is my greatest expectation, and I won't take anything else."

Glen
What's happening today with regard to kindness?

Saratheresa
I'm not going to blame social media, but I think people on the computer are relentless. Seems like people don't mind biting each other's head off and saying the nastiest things anonymously. It has been that way for years, way before COVID. But it feels like people are turning off their ability to be kind. So, things that you hesitated to say before … it's just right there at the forefront: people being critical and expressing themselves at other people's expense, far more readily than they were in the past. Behaviorally, I never had to deal with that before, but I deal with that now.

Glen

I just want to give you an example. I remember when Reagan was president and there were a lot of things people objected to. Let's say it was abortion, the Bitburg cemetery fiasco, Iran-Contra. There was a massive deficit increase, terrorist bombing in Beirut, Lebanon. But I never thought of the president as demonic. Disagree with him? Sure. But the conversations were amiable. We could disagree without killing each other. Now, and I feel sad when talking about this, I feel an invisible barricade in conversation. And it deflates me. Could you respond to any of that as it relates to what's happening now?

Saratheresa

During the lockdown from COVID-19, I heard from parents that their children were getting freaked out by what was on the news: the deaths that were happening all over the country, the flooded hospitals, and the arguments that people had about masking. I realized a lot of children were getting stressed out. I wondered if some of that was because of algorithms feeding them really scary stuff.

I remember discussing this with my children, because they noticed that once they watched one reel on a social media site, all the reels were similar. We had to have discussions about how algorithms work and how their feeds were impacted. If you click on something you find emotional, either in a good way or bad way, you will find more and more content from a similar vantage point, which feeds into fears, anger, or frustrations. This happened to my children and the children of many friends, as well as adults I know. The algorithms are very powerful, but understanding how they work empowers us.

Glen
Hearing that makes me anxious.

Saratheresa
Well, it can feed into my own anxieties. And the truth is, it's also knowing that we need to change because the world is changing. Just the other day, the second day of school, I got in front of class and began the period as I have many times before, saying, "Ladies and gentlemen..." As soon as I said it, I heard it. A student sighed deeply and was like, "Really?" I felt the sting of judgment. Replaying in my head, it was this slow motion of *"Laaaaddddddddddiiieeeee and Geeennnnnttttlllee..."* I had to recover quickly because my goal is to always be inclusive.

Times change and I have to change with them. Addressing my class as ladies and gentlemen used to be how I showed all my students respect; it was mature sounding. But now it isn't. In that moment, I was like, "Where's my Conttttrooooool-Zzzzzz???????"

Glen
Hysterical

Saratheresa

Thanks! The big idea for me is that everyone shows kindness toward each other in my classroom, and that starts with me.

Charleen Martinelli

My 25-year-long friendship with Charleen has resulted in conversations that are broad and deep, and probably laborious to follow., So I've put in subject headings — they will be in **bold** — to draw attention to key issues we discussed.

Glen
So, Charleen? How do you teach in a chaotic new normal?

Charleen
This is something that would be super beneficial for teachers, because, yeah, we are living, breathing, teaching, working in the midst of a new crazy. For me as an educator, it's about the demands that are made on teachers that have nothing to do with teaching. How many years are you teaching now?

Glen
Twenty-six years in. It's a long time.

Increasing Workload With Digital Technology

Charleen
Yeah, I'm starting my twenty-eighth year and I'm working harder now on things that have nothing to do with what I do in the classroom, that take so much time and paperwork. In a digital world, I'm posting things for kids, busy work instead of researching how I can be better in the classroom.

Glen
What are these responsibilities that suck the life out of you?

Charleen
So they suck the life out of you because years ago, you would do all these fun lessons and then you would put the homework on the board. You would write it up in chalk. Right now you have a website. You're constantly updating. Anything I planned for a week has never happened in twenty-six years, because the kids let me know where we're going. So I'm spending all of this time updating and fixing websites so that everything looks clean and crisp, so kids can understand and go back and look. That's where I'm spending a lot of my time.

Glen
Have you ever gotten flack or have other teachers that you know ever gotten flack for being less than attentive to their website?

Charleen
Oh my goodness, yes.

Glen
So you have this … like a low-level added stress: I have to continually update my website so that I can show the administration and parents or whomever that I'm up to date, because everybody has access to it. So if you set due dates, you may have them in the wrong spot?

Charleen

Those are the things that you're dealing with, as opposed to, "Just look at the freaking board and write it down."

Digital Technology Possibly Contributing to Self-censorship

Glen

So there's another thing that comes to mind when I hear that, which is, if I have to put everything online, I might feel reluctant to really say what I'm doing or I might self-censor. Perhaps teachers who are just trying to get through the day would say, "I'm not even going to touch that."

Charleen

Yeah, because there's an actual document trail of what you're doing. Kids can link to it so parents can open links up to see what you are doing. Oh yeah, I completely understand from your perspective. When you opened this conversation up, that's the polarization piece. I have a friend who is now a supervisor and says, "Thank God I'm not teaching anymore."

I say, "Don't you miss the classroom?"

She says, "Not with what's going on right now."

And she was an amazing, amazing social studies teacher. She said, "God forbid I go down 'this' path [unexpected or big topic] or bring something new into the conversation. I would get phone calls."

Glen

What's interesting about you, Charleen, is that you have experience as a vice principal and teacher. Hearing about your friend saying, gosh, I'm so glad I'm not in the classroom, does that experience as an administrator at all contribute to your view that we're in a bit of a new crazy?

For example, does this at all connect to the mental health issues of young people?

The Importance of Grit and Struggle

Charleen

Oh gosh, yes. That's a very big question you're asking. There are so many ways I can answer that. As an administrator, let's start with the mental health piece. So we're living in a society where people lack coping skills. People are afraid to feel negative stuff. People are afraid to hurt. People don't want to be in pain, whether it's physical pain or emotional pain.

Glen

What's wrong with not wanting to feel pain?

Charleen

You can't get away with it, because my thing is, if you're going to love, you're going to lose, you're going to be in pain, and you're going to hurt. Let's take it all in. And we're a society that doesn't do that. We're a society that says, "I don't want you to suffer. I don't want you to struggle." I'm like, "Why not? Why not allow kids to fall flat on their faces. You're going to be OK. The lesson is in getting back up in the face of adversity."

Glen
So we have a society that overvalues "happiness," i.e., a pain-free life, at the expense of living a full life?

Charleen
Yeah, because if you're not happy, something's wrong with you. And that's wrong.

Glen
How?

Charleen
Because now, if kids struggle, they literally melt, crash, and burn. If, God forbid, something's hard, "Oh, my God, if I don't get it this second, then I'm a failure," as opposed to wanting kids to struggle, wanting to keep trying and doing hard things, and valuing struggle: "I know it's hard. Of course, it's supposed to be hard. Life is not easy. So anything you really want is not going to come easily." That's just a huge piece. Value the struggle.

Glen
As an administrator, did you find that teachers were finding that to be a difficult thing to balance?

Charleen
Oh gosh, yes. Teachers are spending a lot of time ... you're in conversations with guidance counselors and parents

because kids are anxious, like, "I have two tests today. So I'm not coming to school because I could fail. I have to get an A, and if I don't, it's over." But if you think about the messaging. Yeah, parents want their kids to get As on everything. And I remember saying to a parent, were you good at everything? And the mother looked at me like I was crazy. It is so competitive today, and that competitiveness does not bring out the best in anybody.

Glen

I just heard something yesterday that was, I thought, brilliant. This mathematician who became a historian applies mathematical models to huge data sets for different civilizations to predict the future. And he says the problem with our society right now is that it's not just competitive; it's hypercompetitive. It's too competitive. When things get too competitive, people cheat. I imagine it leads to mental health challenges, too.

Mental Health Crisis and Students Being Overwhelmed

Charleen

When you're an administrator, you see a lot of things, such as kids being hospitalized because of their mental states. You know, some kids are suicidal. I think it's a contributor. But is it everything? No, because the shitstorm is larger than that. There's the brainwashing of social media, that what they're seeing is absorbing and delusional. Yes, it's hypercompetitive to look the most popular. And there's also a cheating crisis. The kids are so good at it. And students barely have any time to sleep. I can't get mad at a kid for cheating on something because many are already up until 1 a.m. The expectations are so unrealistic. They're actually cruel. What are we doing to our kids? We're setting them up for failure in the worst ways.

Glen

What does that look like? Because as a teacher, I think my course is important. I assign the homework and I think that this is going to enrich their understanding and hopefully their life. But in the aggregate...

Charleen

And they want to. And when they're with you, I'm sure they're actually having the time of their lives. But just think about it. I'm thinking about my classroom as I'm answering this. I ask my kids, "Be with me. Put your stuff away and just be with me. Be here. Be present. Let's do this. Fifty-six minutes is the time that we have." But the minute that bell rings, they're off to the next thing. They don't have time to process what they just did for 56 minutes with me. Now they have to get their mind shifted to come into your classroom, and be present with you, and take in all that information. And then we send them out again. And you have four minutes to get to the next class and do the same thing. We do that at least six times a day, over and over again, day after day. Where's the time to even process what we've learned?

Then they have their after-school stuff, debating, theater, athletics. They have all that and then, finally, they get home at 8 at night. Now they can take a look at what they did at 8 a.m., staying up until 11 p.m., sometimes midnight, to get their work done.

The Importance of Having Time to Reflect or "Stop"

Glen
If I could summarize in one word how to get through today's new crazy, it would be this: Stop.

Charleen
Just stop. Just stop. That's it.

Let's talk about that. I'm just thinking … anytime I go for a golf lesson, I sit in my car and I record notes afterward on what I learned. I do it all the time. After every one of my coaching sessions, I take notes on who I coached and what happened. I sit and reflect. I have the time.

We need to create time for kids to reflect. If we want them to do anything, if we want them to stop cheating, if we want them to stop worrying about getting a 100 on everything, we need to give them time to sit and reflect. You're right. Just stop. Because my thing is, if you give them that time to reflect, you'll probably also get through your content faster because they'll make better connections, new and old.

My thing is, lead with love. That's half the battle.

I have a friend who works at the deli counter over at Kings right down the street. Love her. One of my favorite humans on the planet: spiritual, loves God, and I love her. So when my husband passed away, they were all calling me and praying with me. And it was just beautiful. So to me it's like we're connected; we have a connection. I met her because she would slice my deli meat for me. That's how we got to be friends. And, you know, I went and celebrated something at her church, because they were honoring her. So Todd and I went to see her there, and it was awesome.

But that's what I'm saying. Just lead with love, and you will be able to connect to others. Say hi to people. Say hello. When you meet people, ask, "What is your name?" I want to know your name: you, the person behind the counter. It's letting people know, I see you. I acknowledge you. I value you, because you are a fellow human. I think if we did more of that, it would clean up this mess. I mean, maybe we're not getting out of it, but we'll have each other to get through it.

The Crucial Role of Creating a Climate of Trust

Glen
Amen. How does this play out in the classroom, if it does at all?

Charleen
You have to establish a connection with your kids. The more open you are, the more vulnerable you are with them. It's everything. And then yes, in my math

classroom, yeah, we'll talk about relationships. We'll talk about social media, all kinds of stuff, because those conversations organically come up. There are times when you can pull something from the outside world.

Relationships are everything. Trust is everything. It's a natural progression. When your kids love and respect you, they'll work for you even in a subject they might not be fans of. They'll love coming to your class, because you've created a space, an environment where they can be themselves. So when you think about how to teach today, it comes down to connection. It comes down to relationships. It is the most important thing above all else. If we can carve out those spaces for our kids, then yeah, truth be told, "It's not what they learned in your classroom. It's how they felt when they were with you — how you made them feel." Not my quote, but a good one. That's literally what it comes down to.

And if you can bestow other amazing skills where they walk out of your classroom, where they're better researchers, ask more questions, where they're tenacious, then you've gone above and beyond. I've had kids get so mad at me for pushing them hard but then thanking me. They would say, "Why are you pushing me so hard?" I'm like, because I know you can do it. Because I believe in you. Because you got this. Because when you get it, you're gonna be jumping up and down like a puppy. So once you've established that rapport, the learning begins.

**Two-Minute Speeches with No Notes in a Math Class
And the Importance of Interdisciplinary Curricula**

Glen
Yeah, I mean, could you imagine how boring the classroom would be if it were easy?

I have a dream that teachers can take a societal problem and use course content to address it. I'll give you an example. Let's say you're talking about COVID-19. There's a lot of mathematical ways that you could describe it. You could talk about it in terms of rate of transmission. You could talk about it in terms of calculus, in terms of how far the germs travel, the efficacy of masking.

So let's say that one kid is an anti-masker, hypothetically, and another kid isn't. Great. Create a mathematical proof and discuss it via a two-minute speech, no notes. Use math to make your point. On day one a student says, "This is the truth as I see it." On day two another student says, "No, this is how I see it." They use the math you taught to make their case. Is that idea insane? We can also analyze sources for reliable data, etc. Am I on crack with this?

Charleen
No. It's brilliant. And again, it draws out yet another issue in education. Why are we segregated as subjects? What you just brought up just combined math, science, history, and English. And then we can get into the artistry of it, and we can get into graphic design and how we want those things to look. We have an entire interdisciplinary unit. Education is so compartmentalized. And if you think

about it, the richness of something as simple and complex as COVID-19 — the things that kids could get out of it. You have a debate — now students can improve their public speaking. You're talking about mathematics and the science behind the issues that you interrogate and discuss collectively. You articulate your understanding of the data in a way that makes sense to those around you. That way they can form their own opinion, develop it. Now we can create a civil discussion about the world. There's so much richness with an interdisciplinary perspective. I've been talking about that since I was, like, 25 years old. Back then I asked repeatedly, why can't we do a project together?

Glen
What's that like for administrators?

Charleen
They see the roadblocks. So many roadblocks, because it's a scheduling thing, and then people are going to lose jobs, and then there are so many little components that come into it, like what about the classroom space? So if you're going to be doing this interdisciplinary stuff and you can only hold thirty kids, you can't have five teachers with thirty kids. I understand the variables that they're contending with: getting room space, getting the scheduling right, which is a nightmare. From an administrative perspective, it's hard. It's so complex.

But math is just fascinating on its own. Just standing on its own two legs is sexy and delicious. And if that passion comes through, kids are all in.

Giving Tests in the Beginning of the Unit for Math Classes

Glen

Here's a question: Is my idea of putting the test first applicable to teaching math. The idea is that you give a test first that students work on collaboratively. At the end of class they can see how they did with an answer key provided. Then students take the same test the next day. The test is hard but it starts a conversation among students. They're teaching each other the material. By mastering these tests, they can then become conversational with the material as they try to connect course material to larger topics such as societal problems and such. Is this crazy?

Charleen

I could actually see myself throwing a test at them now being like, this is what you're supposed
to know and then segue into a project. That's a beautiful segue. I could see it being done in a calculus class. So I'm thinking out loud: The more complex the math becomes, the easier it becomes to do what you're suggesting. I was actually thinking about geometry. It would be difficult. But maybe you could do something artistic with it. You could do something with engineering or physics. It is

definitely possible. I just don't think it could be done all the time.

But I also think you could make people nervous because people want things to fit the model exactly. But then I respond, life isn't the exact model. I'm thinking of charting data, like, is that a scattered model? An exponential model? Is that a linear model? Is that a quadrant? "What is that?" You know? You could easily invite kids, but they need to learn the models. But I think the way you're describing how to do it is so much richer, and it really does bring everything in.

Glen
But it makes people nervous, probably especially in math.

The Challenges of State Testing

Charleen
Well yes, we're tested, don't forget. It's the inherent pressure of math. State testing. Constant state testing from K to 12.

Glen
So that reduces such possibilities of applying what you learn.

Charleen
Yeah, it does and it feels counterproductive to me. Teachers think, "That's on the test, so I want my kids to have it." I understand stakeholders need to find benchmarks to see where kids are, but spending more

time on making connections and making things that are not perfect fits, such as learning to fit data to a model would be better.

Also, I understand 100% of what you're saying, but to go from 1 + 1 to the model you speak of, it's complex. It's like, bye. Have a nice day.

Glen
So what I'm hearing is that my approach to this is a little bit fanciful because first of all, state testing is killing...

Charleen
...is such a pain in the ass. It certainly hinders, yes.

Glen
Because they have to teach ABCDEFG. In response to a student saying, "Why do I need to know this?" It's because, well, my rehiring has to do with your test score.

Charleen
Well, this is a stock answer that math teachers give, "The state test." I think we can do better, because math teaches you how to think in a different way. But teaching to a test does not show students why math is important. It's just "Stick to the content." It's made so literal. Of course, math can be literal, exact. And yet, it's not. You can make math subjective. You can have fun with it big time. After ten years of teaching, I finally understood that. Because I was too busy not getting it wrong for the first ten years or being petrified of saying, "I don't know."

Glen

But is my cynical response somewhat accurate? The underlying truth is, this is a tested subject. My hiring is probably dependent upon how students score. If I'm going to start taking chances, like an oddball, scores might suffer. So I'm disincentivized from experimenting in teaching math. And if I play it straight and kids do well, then I'm more reassured of rehiring. So the system says play it straight. Don't take risks. Don't do projects.

The Problem of Teaching in Isolation

Charleen

Yes. And some teachers say, "I'm going my route anyway."

Glen

And how do the conformists learn from the nonconformists and vice versa?

Charleen

That's a great question. I don't know the answer.

Glen

Because I imagine those who do and those who don't probably don't know what the other one does.

Charleen

Well, that's the other thing. We don't get to see each other in action. When you do it's like, wow, what a great idea! Oh, I love what you did there! We don't get enough of that.

School is not about Stop. Slow down. Reflect. For us as teachers, we sweep out the first crew and get in the next crew. Sweep out. Come in. There's no time for colleagues to reflect and see what others are doing. That was one of my favorite parts of when I was an assistant principal. Seeing all the great things going on in classrooms. For the newbies, I might say, "I recommend you go see these teachers. We'll get you coverage. We'll take away a duty for you so you can go see such-and-such in action."

Glen
So you might have a real adventurous math teacher who gets great scores on the state test but still is making it meaningful and dynamic, but other teachers don't learn from that person, and vice versa. It's kind of hush-hush.

Charleen
Yep.

Afterword

I remember the last day of my student teaching (to get certification) back in May 1997. Kids were buzzing from summer weather while teachers looked gloomy and lost.

One moment stood out: A veteran teacher walked past me in the hallway with a face flush from exhaustion and a posture that hung like a question mark about to topple. Then another teacher confided in me (or was he advising?): "You have to understand, students are the enemy. Once you get that, you can teach."

That scary baptism into public school teaching was overwhelming. I would stay at school way past dusk to finish my lesson planning and grading, as though fearing failing in the very place that really failed me: my first-grade classroom in my hometown, a mere 5 miles away.

I remember freezing in front of students the first time I taught a class — tough crowd. But I made "lemonade." The department chair would later write a letter of recommendation that would get me my first teaching job. She said to me constantly, "Survive and advance." Twenty-six years later, her wisdom still resonates.

I began writing this book a year ago. Much has happened since the sky turned orange on June 8, 2023. Headlines now scream from war zones in Gaza and Israel. College campuses are flooded with protests against

Israel's war. I also see signs and billboards around town to "Bring them home," demanding that Hamas release its hostages. The upcoming presidential election promises to bring more chaos. Trump on trial in New York City is surreal.

It's a lot.

Teaching is a lot.

But here we are, teaching in chaotic times.

Yes, we face many of the same challenges that teachers confronted back in 1997. Many students are still ebullient at the thought of a first date. Many weep through adolescence. Most parents still want their children to succeed. Knock-knock jokes still bring chuckles — kinda. And most children still want to experience success in the classroom, even if the distractions of youth water down their results.

Yet today's addictive streaming content overwhelms us in ways that newspapers and TV of 1997 did not. Those newspapers had an "off" switch, because they were published only once a day. In my youth, many television stations stopped broadcasting past midnight.

I talked with my former department chair about the changes that I've been sensing. He taught at River Dell for 45 years and got his PhD because of his love for history, exclaiming it was a great experience: both the teaching and scholarship. He is still spry in his 80s.

I described the crises I saw to him.

He responded, "I taught for 45 years. Best time of my life! Enjoy it!"

I asked, "When did you retire?"

He said, "In 2007."

I asked, "The very year that all students got laptops? The same year the digital revolution flooded into our school?"

"Oh," he said.

In 1962, the year my former boss began teaching, the VHS video cassette tape wasn't even invented. Phones were still rotary, and TVs were black and white.

It was like my boss and I spoke from two different eras: his from the Industrial Revolution, mine from the Digital on the cusp of another, the AI Revolution.

It's hard to navigate when your map changes by the minute. My boss navigated teaching for 45 years partly because his map didn't change that much in the classroom. But now, well, it's different. When I floated my initial book title to teachers, those whom I had known and those whom I'd met in passing, they exclaimed with near universal acclaim, like someone was saying what they were thinking for a long time, "Yes! Thank you!" That title was, "How to Teach in a Sh*tstorm," so titled because that's often how it felt.

One thing has provided me solace. My department chair, Lisa Torres, has invited me to lead professional development workshops called GLAM (Growth, Learning, Assessment Mindset). It's a group of educators interested in thinking outside the box and helping each other grow.

Also, Lisa has invited me to be a guest lecturer in her college classes. These opportunities have given me an impetus to research more deeply into the science of learning; they have also expanded my audience. I'm starting to teach teachers.

This new journey I call Glen 2.0: Teachers play "Heads, Shoulders, Knees, Toes" before wrestling with big questions; Glen preaches like an evangelist to fail forward with a smile and knock-knock jokes.

To thrive today, we need to speak with other teachers about teaching. We need actionable steps to help get us through the day. And we need to give each other the stage to ask the questions that haunt us, "How do I teach well without sacrificing weekends grading?" Or, "How do I get students to care?" Or, "How do I prevent burnout?" Approaching such questions with seriousness and rigor will help teachers reclaim their voice; in doing so, we'll encourage students to use theirs. This process can help restore our democracy and civility.

I still can't shake the despondency I sometimes feel, that education is too slow a process in a world that is changing so fast. I still wonder how a lesson plan can address such problems.

The answer is, of course, in asking big questions and daring to listen:

"What do you see?"

"What do you think?"

"What should we do?"

It's in the listening that we create community, which will be crucial for all of us in the years ahead.

Reach out to me to continue the conversation.

A brief word of thanks: Rebecca Henderson, thank you for being an ally throughout the writing process of this book, of rewriting, reimagining, and supporting me the whole way through. You're the best teacher anyone could ask for. It's because of you that I've been able to write a book of which I am proud. Heartfelt thank you.

Thank you, Daryl, my love. I still can't find my socks. I think *Mayhem* took them... or was it Mischief?

Appendices

Appendix I:
"What Would 'X' Say?"

Published in the *NJEA Review*, February 2023

I have taught social studies for 25 years. I believe that it's not enough to know something; students must be able to use what they know to make something new as well as to see the world in new and interesting ways. I do this with social studies, but I believe the following question can inspire learning in any classroom: "What would X say?"

"X" is the thought or person who brings your course to life.

Here are some examples

- What would Gandhi say about driverless cars?
- What would George Washington say about COVID-19?
- What would Galileo say about the James Webb Space Telescope?
- What would Picasso say about Instagram?
- What would Michelangelo say about Photoshop?
- What would Martin Luther King Jr. say about our elections?
- What would Henry Ford say about Happy Meals?
- What would Helen Keller say about Title IX?

- What would our Founding Fathers say about Trump's impeachment?

Here's some background on the last question: It was the fall of 2019. President Donald Trump was being investigated in the House of Representatives for leveraging U.S. relations with Ukraine to sway the 2020 presidential election. So we debated this question: "What would our Founding Fathers say about President Trump's alleged involvement in the Ukraine?" Students then chose a Founding Father and argued whether they would be for President Trump's impeachment.

In this instance X was the Founding Fathers. We used their views to help us understand the day's big issues, which in this case was the question of Trump's impeachment.

It brought class to life. It energized students to express their unique ideas. Furthermore, it energized me. When we used history as a tool to help us better understand the complex issue of impeachment, the classroom became a place of genuine inquiry.

I remember one student who got the class to stop and think. She asked, "But is it enough? What is the line at which we determine whether to throw out our president — an elected official? Is one phone call enough?"

It was a great question that motivated students to research more deeply and evaluate what our founders thought about the rule of law, the power of mobs, the corrosive effects of power, and the fear of foreign interference in our politics.

After the assignment I surveyed students: Was it worthwhile for us to have learned about the founders by looking at it through the lens of Trump and his impeachment? Eighty-eight percent of students said "Yes." Twelve percent said "No." This response from one student echoed throughout many of the 67 respondents who answered the survey:

"*I believe it was worthwhile because I think all young adults should be exposed to current events as much as possible. We are the next generation of adults, and we're 15-16 years old, which means we will be voting soon. By being knowledgeable about our current president and what he's doing and the decisions he is making, we as citizens will become more well-versed in how we want our country to be run.*"

When students are afforded numerous opportunities — to try, fail, learn from each other, and try again — when students tackle challenging, open-ended questions like "What would X say?" we all get energized.

This type of question can enrich your classroom.

Appendix II:
"Two Minutes to Mastery: Climbing the Mountain of Public Speaking"

Published in the *NJEA Review,* February 2022

I believe at the center of meaningful teaching is asking students, "What do you think?" and listening to their answers. When we use course content to better understand our world, we get outside of our comfort zone and grow personally and professionally.

I try to hit that target with an end-of-unit assessment that I call Two Minutes to Mastery. Students complete two-minute speeches with no notes. In the best sense, it scares students; it causes them to band together, hear divergent points of view, learn from each other, and work as a team. My goal is for students to complete that challenging task in a workshop setting and use course content to deepen their insights about their world.

The task begins with students addressing challenging prompts. I call them Shangri-la prompts, because they lead us to good places. The prompts require applying course content to our world today. As a social studies teacher, I have asked these kinds of questions [All assigned before June 8, 2023]:

- What Enlightenment ideal (e.g. democracy, trial by jury, rule of law, election) needs an update so as to avoid another January 6 raid on the capitol?

- What lesson should the Venezuelans or their government learn from the French Revolution to avoid further calamity?
- Should Andrew Jackson stay on the twenty-dollar bill?
- To what extent is China's presence in Angola imperialism?
- How did African American music help end segregation in the South?

These questions require students to show mastery of course content and, as importantly, use it to better understand their world. It's not easy: students need to know what happened on Jan. 6, 2021, need to know what is happening in Venezuela today, need to understand current events in Africa with regard to China's presence there, need to wrestle with the legacy of Andrew Jackson, and need to appreciate the historic impact of African American music on the United States.

I believe good questions can spur interest in any topic: math, science, music, language arts, and on and on. It starts with silence ... on the other side of the question mark. If I ask, "What do you think?" allow perfect silence, and care enough to listen, that's when the learning starts. That's the opportunity.

I want to give you courage. Don't think of your subject as calcified. Your subject is dynamic, new, and *now*.

If our intention is to grow, we must ask inspired questions. Do so with this North Star: "I don't know, but I will find out with you." Yes, math, too, evolves. Take, for example, geometry, with its 2,000-year-old proofs. When we insert the world into the curriculum, the statue steps down from its pedestal. It draws a breath. It's no longer an inanimate object confined to a museum.

Two Minutes to Mastery must get students to think, stretch their limitations, communicate, fail, and feel excited about participation. In short, I want it to catalyze the creation of community, the kind that inspires growth. Early in my teaching career, one of my students cried because I told her to do her speech again. The girl was brilliant and a perfectionist, but she was thrown off by my request. The room got very tense very quickly, but a touch of humor defused the emotion. Soon, everyone, including the girl, was laughing in a hysterical, joyful way. We were learning that we could do better than "one and done," getting only a single shot at a project or performance. "One and done" is a lot of weight to carry that often undoes heartfelt effort.

Instead, we can workshop, get critical feedback from peers, improve, and eventually create something really good by any measure, for college and beyond. The student who got emotional over her grade later delivered an amazing and powerful speech because she felt empowered by not being bound by a single performance. Ultimately, do-overs allow a class to improve when the bar is high and the intention to improve is genuine, when opportunities to try again are real and the topic engages.

Many adults can't speak for two minutes in an organized, compelling, and informed fashion about the complexities of current events. It takes practice, failure, overcoming stage fright, and a supportive audience/team. But when we do the work, a feeling of empowerment emerges.

Speeches are generally delivered from the back of the room, a space typically not associated with where speeches are traditionally delivered. All desks are pushed to the front of the room, except for one. I push one desk against the wall in the back of the room. The speaker can then sit on that desk to deliver their speech. This reduces stress.

I position myself between six and ten feet away, seated to their right at a desk by the wall, taking notes as each student speaks. If prompted, I may offer suggestions. Students do the same. We create a big U shape around the speaker. In chairs only, we sit close to the speaker, creating an intimate atmosphere. Each student has only a notebook, a pen, and perhaps a printed copy of what I handed out previously concerning the expectations for the speech. We're now ready to help.

By the time students present their speeches, they have already researched for at least a day, brainstormed with me for another day, researched with the librarian to learn more deeply about the topic, and spent a day writing their scripts.

Generally, one student volunteers to go first. (There's usually someone who wants to get it over with.) Within a minute, speakers realize it's far less stressful than imagined, even though expectations remain high.

When someone volunteers, I comment on one of the four outlined expectations:

1. Content mastery (showing a balanced understanding of course content and societal issues).
2. Thematic coherence (when an idea, insight, or suggestion is argued throughout the presentation)
3. Organized presentation (talking about each topic in detail — no switching back and forth — in thoughtful, organized, and well-developed paragraphs)
4. Unique insight and research (no repeating other students' answers).

Our goal is to get students organized, lucid, and conversant with the material. Together students develop an informal, confident command of the material as each student sits on that desk and tells us what they think. This requires students to become comfortable speaking to the class. They receive feedback and try again. If a student is tongue-tied, no worries. We can discuss alternative approaches. If the theme doesn't work, students brainstorm ideas or facts to elevate their game.

In other words, on the first go-round, we workshop. We dissect and get a collective sense of what sounds right, mindful that each student needs to present a unique point of view — no parroting. If someone speaks impressively, we acknowledge it. If a speaker sounds lifeless, as if a speech has been memorized, we'll say, "Say what you think. Don't recite a script."

The whole point of speaking without a script — or with only twenty words of notes — is to get students comfortable. This may seem counterintuitive, but a script kills the engagement. The notecard with only twenty words raises the bar. It demands focus and the creation of something meaningful.

Students present speeches that are impressive in various ways — serious, witty, soft spoken, dramatic, or authoritative. There are many ways up the mountain, but to summit we must show command of the topic: 1) argue coherently, 2) be organized, 3) informed, and 4) present a unique point of view.

When we give students the opportunity to say what they think, research deeply, use course content to promote divergent thinking, and learn in community with multiple attempts at mastery, the classroom becomes a powerful place indeed.

What has made Two Minutes to Mastery successful?

1. The high bar that might have seemed intimidating at first but rallies the class
2. The teacher who cares and appreciates the difficulty of the task
3. The common purpose that provides an incentive for students to work together
4. The workshop format, which helps make the goal attainable
5. Most importantly, real opportunities to "fail gloriously," try again, and learn with feedback from their classmates and teacher

Appendix III: "Reinventing Testing"

Published in the *NJEA Review*, February 2021

Testing needs to be reinvented. Instead of one-and-done paper-pencil testing, repurposed computer-based testing software can help transform the classroom into a student-centered, collaborative experience.

The chart below distinguishes traditional versus collaborative low-stakes testing. When teachers leverage online testing's superpower — instant feedback — students can better strategize ways to succeed, and teachers can better craft lessons that create relevance between content and students' interests.

Let's define tests in my class. They are basically 10-point assignments that codify course content; they could be as rigorous as a final exam but can be retaken until mastery. My initial expectation is generally 100; yet expectations may vary by class and context.

Traditional Test	Collaborative Low-Stakes Testing
Test is taken at the end of a unit.	Test is taken at the beginning of a unit.

Test is taken once. Students don't get feedback until the teacher returns the test.	Test taken as many times as needed to gain mastery, perhaps a 100. Feedback is immediate via computer-generated answer key. Students work together to figure it out.
Test questions tend to be straightforward, high stakes, and (perhaps) not so imaginative. If you get it wrong, you lose points.	Test questions can convey a narrative, compel conversations, or stimulate debates. Points earned after a specific score demonstrate mastery.
Heavily weighted test grade. This supposedly incentivizes students to study but has the potential to stifle their voice.	Not a heavily weighted grade, 10 points+/-. Students help each other throughout the "test taking" experience. They self-advocate, ask for help, and participate in an "all boats rise" culture.
The test is a static document.	The test is a living document that students and teachers can revise in real time.

Once a test is completed, answers are perhaps forgotten and relevance suffers.	Repetition reinforces content knowledge. Additionally, once students complete the test, they can apply that knowledge to answer real-world questions/contemporary issues. (See Venezuela project below.)

My "Collaborative Low-Stakes Tests" are taken in the beginning of a unit. Students work on them in small groups and are encouraged to teach each other the answers. If a student gets an answer wrong, they can take the test again. This repetition helps develop grit and deepens content mastery. If not completed in a class period, it can be retaken at lunch, correcting only the questions that were wrong. Yes, students can bring a friend. The next day, I may require them to retake the same test without notes, independently. Again, this is not tied to a heavily weighted grade.

Repurposing testing software can elevate the questions that are tested. Instead of simply asking, for example, "Who is Louis XVI?" in a lecture format, students can now construct the story you want them to know. This can happen when we reimagine how to ask questions and how to leverage the power of immediate feedback in test-taking software. For example, when teaching the French Revolution, I might ask questions like the ones below.

1. _____Louis XVI	A. The first one being that he lived in a gilded cage known as Versailles, which isolated him from his people.
2. _____There were numerous problems with his leadership style	
3. _____This palace would become so lavish	B. Was a young and inexperienced king who was unprepared to face France's numerous crises, which would end his reign.
4. _____All the while the printing press	C. Spread news of the king's lavish consumption, a message he could not squash.
	5. D. That it became an object of scorn where the king "devoured the people's substance," so said Robespierre.

Correct answers: 1 = B; 2 = A; 3 = D, 4 = C

The matching section above is just one example of a dozen such questions I might ask to help students comprehend and appreciate larger themes. Again, I can revise expectations as students give feedback in real time.

If a question confuses, we can edit them in class as they take the "test." We can create questions together before test day.

I generally craft questions to attack different levels of Bloom's Taxonomy and found that different question types are suitable for different kinds of analysis. For example: matching questions are useful to drive storytelling; multiple-correct-answer formats help spur analysis of primary sources; true/false choices can motivate close reading; multiple choice are good for recalling basic information.

But more important than students learning about the French Revolution, I want them to understand issues of the French Revolution in a 2020 context. So, in my testing, I create charts that require students to compare the history to contemporary issues: income inequality, national budgets and deficits, taxation policy, maps of foreign wars, and political cartoons. Through the test, we become fluent not just with basic history. We also become informed about what is happening in our world today. Furthermore, we use history to help us better understand our world.

Revising a test is as easy as projecting it on a screen for all to see; we can modify it together. This gives students a voice, autonomy, clarity of purpose, and helps forge a growth mindset and culture of collaboration. Now, most importantly, we can use this information for more inspired learning, such as our project on Venezuela, which required students to research beyond the test and make their own meaning from what they learned.

In the 2019-20 school year, my colleagues and I developed what I believe was an inspired end-of-unit assessment on the French Revolution. Worth a test grade of 50 points, students were tasked with delivering two-minute speeches with no notes on this prompt: "Based on your understanding of the French Revolution, what can be done so that Venezuela avoids its own violent revolution?"

We Skyped with a Venezuelan family who was living in Venezuela at the time. We asked them what they thought could be done to avoid Venezuela's collapse. It resulted in memorable conversations indeed. It galvanized me, my colleagues, and our students to donate money and more than 250 pounds of food and medical supplies to the family. They responded with a cellphone video of their singing "Amazing Grace" and "Guantanamera" to us.

The topic became urgent, profound, and required action; the history gave context to our conversation. This was facilitated by the formative test that the students took at the start of the unit. It made the topic accessible, meaningful, and relevant.

After students Skyped, they crafted and delivered two-minute speeches with no notes. They delivered them at least twice, once with peer review by all classmates, the other time one-on-one with me.

Afterward, I surveyed students and asked how they found the three-pronged approach, which consisted of:

1. Taking the test collaboratively
2. Retaking it individually

3. Applying their knowledge to Venezuela's turmoil

Ninety-two percent of students said they thought the system worked and identified different reasons. Some liked the clarity of expectations of the test, that it explained material clearly or spurred collaboration; several appreciated that they could retry until mastery. What I liked was the fact that the test did not count as a test. They only count five points when taken collaboratively, and ten points when taken individually. Their need to succeed was constructed through peer motivation.

Here is a sample of what students are saying about the three-pronged approach:

- I think 100-or-Nothing Quia [online "tests" at Quia.com] is better, because you really have to know the material to pass. To get 100 on them, you have to take it multiple times to get 100, which in my opinion, is better, because you better understand the material each time you take the Quia.
- Doing the 100-or-Nothings are good practice. It is even better when we have the "test" the next day because the information is still fresh in our minds, so it is easier to take it [take test once, no notes, independently]. I have never been a fan of essays, but I do think they are good to learn new/more information about the topic.

- I feel as though the system has been working for me, although the essays can be a stretch at times. They are in fact fun to write, but sometimes they confuse me. I feel as if we spent one more day going over the 100-or-Nothing, I can retain the most important information. The essays are fun at times and bring new topics to the class, which is interesting to hear.
- I like doing an essay or discussing a larger question because then I know where I'm at with my understanding. But I don't want to do an essay for every single topic.
- I think that the system is good, because you learn by doing the 100-or-Nothing. Then, you get tested on what you remember. Then you expand your knowledge about interesting, real world topics.

One-and-done end-of-unit testing limits learning. Let's reinvent tests so that they serve as a formative yet crucial step toward student empowerment.

To get started, employ a good web-based, test-taking program with the qualities listed below. I like Quia.com.

1. It is important to have the option to change when students can see the answer key. Ninety-nine percent of the time, I want students to see the entire test and answer key at the beginning of a unit.
2. As teachers, you want the flexibility to randomize question order.

3. Make sure your testing application allows you to easily insert graphics, such as maps, art, charts, political cartoons, or excerpts from books.

4. Students need to be able to access all their tests so that they can identify what they got wrong.

5. The more question types available the better. These are helpful: matching, fill-in-blank for a paragraph (not just a sentence), multiple correct answers.

6. Time stamps are helpful. They can provide a metric of work ethic of when a student studied, how many times they attempted a test, and for how long they worked.

7. In an online environment, we have to be creative.

Made in United States
North Haven, CT
02 May 2025

68513725R00117